Skills Worksheet)

Directed Reading A

Section: Currents

1. Oceans contain streamlike movements of water known

as ____________________.

2. Currents are influenced by weather, the Earth's ____________________,

and the position of the ____________________.

ONE WAY TO EXPLORE CURRENTS

3. From where to where did Thor Heyerdahl and his crew sail the Kon-Tiki?

____

____

____

4. What theory was Heyerdahl trying to prove by sailing the Kon-Tiki?

____

____

____

SURFACE CURRENTS

5. Horizontal movements of water that occur at or near the ocean's surface are

called ____________________.

6. Compare the directions in which surface currents flow near the poles and
near the equator.

____

____

____

7. Why do wind and surface currents appear to move in curved paths?

____

____

____

Directed Reading A *continued*

8. What is the scientific term for the apparent curved motion of moving objects called?

____

____

____

9. What happens when a surface current meets a continent?

____

____

____

10. Where do cold-water and warm-water currents begin?

____

____

____

DEEP CURRENTS

Match the correct description with the correct term. Write the letter in the space provided.

_______**11.** a streamlike movement of ocean water located far below the surface

_______**12.** the amount of matter in a given space, or volume

_______**13.** a measure of the amount of dissolved salts or solids in a liquid

_______**14.** a process which removes water but leaves solids behind

_______**15.** a measure of how hot or cold something is

a. evaporation

b. deep currents

c. density

d. salinity

e. temperature

16. Why is ocean water denser near the poles?

____

____

____

Directed Reading A *continued*

17. Why does ocean water that is covered by ice increase in density?

____

____

____

18. Why does evaporation increase the density of ocean water?

____

____

____

19. Which is colder, a deep current or a surface current?

____

____

____

20. Which has greater salinity, a deep current or a surface current?

____

____

____

Directed Reading A

Section: Currents and Climate
SURFACE CURRENTS AND CLIMATE

_______ **1.** What land areas are warmed and cooled by surface currents?
   a. areas at the same latitudes
   b. coastal areas
   c. lands in the Tropics
   d. places with mild climates

_______ **2.** Where does the Gulf Stream get its warmth?
   a. from the Tropics
   b. from the North Atlantic
   c. from the British Isles
   d. from Newfoundland

_______ **3.** In what directions does the Gulf Stream flow?
   a. south and west
   b. north and west
   c. north and east
   d. south and east

_______ **4.** Where does the California Current gets it cold water?
   a. along the California coast
   b. from the Tropics
   c. from the Gulf Stream
   d. from the North Pacific Ocean

_______ **5.** In what direction does the California Current flow?
   a. north
   b. south
   c. east
   d. west

_______ **6.** When upwelling takes place, cold water from the deep ocean
   a. moves further out to sea.
   b. causes photosynthesis.
   c. rises to the surface.
   d. gets replaced by warm water.

_______ **7.** Upwelling happens when winds blow surface currents
   a. from north to south.
   b. against their usual direction.
   c. to the sunny surface.
   d. away from the shore.

Directed Reading A *continued*

8. In what ocean do El Niño and La Niña form?

____

____

____

9. How does the surface temperature of the ocean change during El Niño?

____

____

____

10. How does the surface temperature of the ocean change during La Niña?

____

____

____

11. List three disasters that may occur when El Niño changes the weather patterns.

____

____

____

12. Why is it important for scientists to learn as much as possible about El Niño?

____

____

____

13. What four things do the network of NOAA operated buoys record?

____

____

____

____

Directed Reading A

Section: Waves

ANATOMY OF A WAVE

1. Waves are made up of two main parts. The _______________________ is the

highest point of a wave. The _______________________ is the lowest point.

2. The distance between two adjacent wave crests or wave troughs is

the _______________________.

3. The vertical distance between the crest and trough of a wave is called

the _______________________.

WAVE FORMATION AND MOVEMENT

4. What is the source of energy that creates most ocean waves?

____

____

____

5. What happens to water when a wave of energy passes through it?

____

____

____

SPECIFICS OF WAVE MOVEMENT

6. The time between the passage of two wave crests (or troughs) at a fixed point

is called the _______________________.

7. Dividing the wavelength by the wave period gives you

the _______________________.

Directed Reading A *continued*

TYPES OF WAVES

Match the correct description with the correct term. Write the letter in the space provided.

_______ **8.** waves that move in water deeper than one-half their wavelength

_______ **9.** waves that reach water shallower than one-half their wavelength

_______ **10.** waves that crest and then crash into the ocean floor

_______ **11.** area where waves first begin to tumble downward, or break

_______ **12.** the area between the breaker zone and the shore

_______ **13.** a subsurface current that is near the shore and that pulls objects out to sea

_______ **14.** a water current that travels near and parallel to the shoreline

_______ **15.** the bubbles in the crest of a breaking wave

_______ **16.** long rolling waves that move steadily and at long distances across the ocean

_______ **17.** a giant ocean wave that forms after a volcanic eruption, submarine earthquake, or landslide

_______ **18.** a local rise in sea level near the shore, caused by strong winds from a hurricane or other storm

a. breakers

b. deep-water waves

c. longshore current

d. shallow-water waves

e. storm surge

f. surf

g. swells

h. tsunami

i. undertow

j. whitecap

k. breaker zone

Skills Worksheet)

Directed Reading A

Section: Tides

1. What are *tides*?

____

2. What two forces influence tides?

____

____

THE LURE OF THE MOON

Write the letter of the correct answer in the space provided.

_______ **3.** The relationship between the phases of the moon and the tides was
first discovered
  a. by a Greek named Pytheas.
  b. by Sir Isaac Newton.
  c. in 1687.
  d. after gravity was discovered.

_______ **4.** The moon's pull is strongest at the place on Earth that is
  a. opposite the moon.
  b. directly facing the moon.
  c. opposite the sun.
  d. directly facing the sun

_______ **5.** The pull of the moon on the ocean causes water to bulge and create
  a. waves.
  b. the rotation of the Earth.
  c. high tides.
  d. gravity.

_______ **6.** The two factors that determine when tides occur are the rotation of
the Earth and the
  a. rotation of the moon.
  b. revolution of the moon.
  c. rotation of the sun.
  d. location of the sun.

_______ **7.** How long does it take for a spot on Earth that is facing the moon to
rotate so that it is facing the moon again?
  a. 24 h and 5 m   **c.** 12 h and 50 m
  b. 12 h and 5 m   **d.** 24 h and 50 m

TIDAL VARIATIONS

8. The difference in levels of ocean water at high tide and low tide is called

a ________________________.

9. Tides that occur when the sun, moon, and Earth are aligned are

________________________ tides.

10. Tides with the smallest daily tidal range are ________________________ tides.

TIDES AND TOPOGRAPHY

11. What is a *tidal bore*?

____

____

____

____

____

12. Where do tidal bores occur?

____

____

13. What place on Earth has the greatest tidal range?

____

____

Directed Reading B

Section: Currents

Read the words in the box. Read the sentences. <u>Fill in each blank</u> with the word or phrase that best completes the sentence.

continents	water	weather

1. Ocean currents are streamlike movements of ocean

   _________________.

2. Storms and other kinds of _________________ can

   change ocean currents.

3. Ocean currents also change because of the Earth's rotation and

   where the _________________ are located.

ONE WAY TO EXPLORE CURRENTS

<u>Circle the letter</u> of the best answer for each question.

4. Which word BEST describes the *Kon-Tiki*?

   a. current

   b. theory

   c. sailboat

   d. raft

SURFACE CURRENTS

5. Which of the following does NOT control surface currents?

   a. rivers

   b. continental deflections

   c. global winds

   d. the Coriolis effect

Global Winds

6. Close to the poles in what direction is ocean water blown?

   a. east to west

   b. west to east

   c. toward the land

   d. toward the open sea

Directed Reading B *continued*

The Coriolis Effect

Circle the letter of the best answer for each question.

7. In the Coriolis effect, how do currents appear to move?

   a. in curved paths

   b. in straight paths

   c. toward the land

   d. toward the open sea

Continental Deflections

8. What happens to an ocean current when it gets deflected?

   a. It gets cold.

   b. It sinks.

   c. It moves faster.

   d. It changes direction.

Taking Temperatures

9. Where do cold-water currents begin?

   a. near the equator

   b. near the poles

   c. in deep water

   d. in shallow water

DEEP CURRENTS

Read the description. Then draw a line from the dot next to each description to the matching word.

10. a streamlike movement of water that forms deep in the ocean ●

11. the amount of matter in a given space ●

12. the amount of dissolved salts or solids in a liquid ●

   a. deep current

   b. density

   c. salinity

▌Directed Reading B *continued*

Formation and Movement of Deep Currents
<u>Circle the letter</u> of the best answer for each question.

13. What happens to ocean water that is covered by ice?

    a. It gets less dense.

    b. It begins to move.

    c. It gets denser.

    d. It cracks the ice.

14. How does evaporation change the ocean water that is left behind?

    a. The water gets less dense.

    b. The water sinks down.

    c. The water gets denser.

    d. The water gets fresher.

15. How do deep ocean currents compare to surface ocean currents?

    a. Deep currents flow faster.

    b. Deep currents are denser.

    c. Winds directly control deep currents.

    d. Deep currents are less dense.

Directed Reading B

Section: Currents and Climate

SURFACE CURRENTS AND CLIMATE

<u>Circle the letter</u> of the best answer for each question.

1. Which land areas are mostly warmed and cooled by surface currents?

   a. inland areas

   b. coastal areas

   c. mountain areas

   d. the Gulf Stream

Warm-Water Currents and Climate

2. Where does the Gulf Stream gets its warmth?

   a. from the Tropics

   b. from the North Atlantic

   c. from the British Isles

   d. from the Poles

Cold-Water Currents and Climate

3. In what direction does the California Current flow?

   a. north   **c.** east

   b. south   **d.** west

Upwelling

4. In what direction does cold water move during an upwelling?

   a. from north to south

   b. away from the land

   c. toward the ocean surface

   d. toward the ocean floor

Directed Reading B *continued*

El Niño

Read the description. Then <u>draw a line</u> from the dot next to each description to the matching word.

5. how the ocean surface changes during El Niño ●

6. how the ocean surface changes during La Niña ●

7. a long period of time with no rain ●

8. used to collect data to predict an El Niño ●

a. cooler

b. drought

c. buoys

d. warmer

Directed Reading B

Section: Waves
ANATOMY OF A WAVE
Circle the letter of the best answer for each question.

1. What is the highest point of a wave?

   a. crest

   b. trough

   c. wave height

   d. wavelength

2. What is the lowest point of a wave?

   a. crest

   b. trough

   c. wave height

   d. wavelength

3. What is distance between two crests or troughs?

   a. crest

   b. trough

   c. wave height

   d. wavelength

4. What is the vertical distance between a crest and a trough?

   a. crest

   b. trough

   c. wave height

   d. wavelength

WAVE FORMATION AND MOVEMENT

<u>Circle the letter</u> of the best answer for each question.

5. What is the source of energy that creates most ocean waves?

   a. wind   **c.** convection

   b. earthquakes   **d.** water

6. How does water move when a wave of energy passes through it?

   a. forward

   b. backwards

   c. into the air

   d. in a small circle

SPECIFICS OF WAVE MOVEMENT

7. What do you need to figure out wave speed?

   a. wavelength and height

   b. wavelength and wave period

   c. wave energy and time

   d. wavelength

8. What does a wave period measure?

   a. speed of each wave

   b. energy

   c. time between two waves

   d. wavelength

TYPES OF WAVES

9. Which of the following can form waves?

   a. a full moon

   b. impacts by cosmic bodies

   c. the seasons

   d. sunset

Directed Reading B *continued*

Deep-Water Waves and Shallow-Water Waves

Read the description. Then <u>draw a line</u> from the dot next to each description to the matching word.

10. waves that move in water deeper than one-half their wavelength ●

11. waves that move in water shallower than one-half their wavelength ●

12. waves that crest and then crash into the ocean floor ●

13. the area between the breaker zone and the shore ●

a. breakers

b. deep-water waves

c. shallow-water waves

d. surf

Shore Currents

<u>Circle the letter</u> **of the best answer for each question.**

14. Which of the following is a subsurface current that pulls objects out to sea?

   a. tsunami   **c.** undertow

   b. breaker   **d.** longshore current

Longshore Currents

15. What forms after waves hit the beach at an angle?

   a. longshore current   **c.** surf

   b. undertow   **d.** pollution

Open-Ocean Waves

16. Which waves are long, rolling waves in the open ocean?

   a. tsunamis   **c.** whitecaps

   b. longshore currents   **d.** swells

| Directed Reading B *continued*

Circle the letter of the best answer for each question.

17. What do you call the bubbles at the crest of a breaking wave?

   a. tsunamis

   b. longshore currents

   c. whitecaps

   d. swells

Tsunamis

18. Besides earthquakes, what causes tsunamis?

   a. underwater explosions

   b. undertows

   c. longshore currents

   d. storm surges

Storm Surges

19. Which one of the following might cause a storm surge?

   a. tsunami

   b. whitecap

   c. hurricane

   d. swell

Directed Reading B

Section: Tides
THE LURE OF THE MOON
Circle the letter of the best answer for each question.

1. Who first discovered that the tides changed with the moon?

   a. Pytheas

   b. Sir Isaac Newton

   c. scientists

   d. sailors

High Tide and Low Tide

2. On what part of the Earth is the moon's pull the strongest?

   a. the ocean

   b. places that are in daylight

   c. places directly facing the moon

   d. places at angles to the moon

Battle of the Bulge

3. What kind of tides occur when the moon makes the ocean water bulge?

   a. high tides

   b. low tides

   c. spring tides

   d. neap tides

Directed Reading B *continued*

Timing the Tides

Circle the letter of the best answer for each question.

4. How long does it take the moon to revolve around the Earth?

a. one half of a day

b. 24 h and 50 m

c. 24 h

d. 50 m

Tidal Variations

5. What do you measure to figure out the tidal range?

a. spring tides

b. neap tides

c. phases of the moon

d. high and low tides

Spring Tides

6. When do spring tides happen?

a. in the spring

b. during the new and full moons

c. in the third quarter

d. in the fourth quarter

Neap Tides

7. Which phrase describes a neap tide?

a. smallest daily tidal range

c. spring tides

b. largest tidal range

d. tidal range

Tides and Topography

8. What causes a very sudden tidal rise?

a. high tides

c. gravity

b. a tidal range

d. a tidal bore

Vocabulary and Section Summary

Currents

VOCABULARY

In your own words, write a definition of the following terms in the space provided.

1. ocean current

____

____

2. surface current

____

____

3. Coriolis effect

____

____

4. deep current

____

____

SECTION SUMMARY

Read the following section summary.

- Surface currents are streamlike movements of water at or near the surface of the ocean.
- Surface currents are controlled by three factors: global winds, the Coriolis effect, and continental deflections.
- Deep currents are streamlike movements of ocean water located far below the surface.
- Deep currents form where the density of ocean water increases. Water density depends on temperature and salinity.

Vocabulary and Section Summary

Currents and Climate

VOCABULARY

In your own words, write a definition of the following terms in the space provided.

1. upwelling

____

____

2. El Niño

____

____

3. La Niña

____

____

SECTION SUMMARY

Read the following section summary.

- Surface currents affect the climate of the land near which they flow.
- Warm-water currents bring warmer climates to coastal regions.
- Cold-water currents bring cooler climates to coastal regions.
- During El Niño, warm and cool surface waters change locations.
- El Niño can cause floods, mudslides, and drought.

Vocabulary and Section Summary

Waves

VOCABULARY

In your own words, write a definition of the following terms in the space provided.

1. undertow

____

____

2. longshore current

____

____

3. whitecap

____

____

4. swell

____

____

5. tsunami

____

____

6. storm surge

____

____

▌ Vocabulary and Section Summary *continued*

SECTION SUMMARY

Read the following section summary.

- Waves are made up of two main parts—crests and troughs.

- Waves are usually created by the transfer of the wind's energy across the surface of the ocean.

- Waves travel through water near the water's surface, while the water itself rises and falls in circular movements.

- Wind-generated waves are classified as deep-water or shallow-water waves.

- When waves hit the shore at a certain angle, they can create either an undertow or a longshore current.

- Tsunamis are dangerous waves that can be very destructive to coastal communities.

Vocabulary and Section Summary

Tides

VOCABULARY

In your own words, write a definition of the following terms in the space provided.

1. tide

2. tidal range

3. spring tide

4. neap tide

SECTION SUMMARY

Read the following section summary.

- Tides are caused by the gravitational forces of the moon and sun on the Earth.
- The moon's gravity is the main force behind the tides.
- The positions of the sun and moon relative to the position of the Earth cause tidal ranges.
- The four different types of tides are: high tides, low tides, spring tides, and neap tides.

Section Review

Currents

USING KEY TERMS

The statements below are false. For each statement, replace the underlined word to make a true statement.

1. <u>Deep currents</u> are directly controlled by wind.

   ____

2. An increase in density in parts of the ocean can cause <u>surface currents</u> to form.

   ____

   ____

UNDERSTANDING KEY IDEAS

_________ 3. Surface currents
   - **a.** are formed by wind.
   - **b.** are streamlike movements of water.
   - **c.** can travel across entire oceans.
   - **d.** All of the above

4. List three factors that control surface currents.

   ____

   ____

   ____

5. How does a continent affect the movement of a surface current?

   ____

   ____

   ____

6. Explain how temperature and salinity affect the formation of deep currents.

   ____

   ____

   ____

Section Review *continued*

MATH SKILLS

7. The Gulf Stream flows along the North Carolina coast at 90 million cubic meters per second and at 40 million cubic miles per second when it turns eastward. How much faster is the Gulf Stream flowing along the coast than when it turns eastward? Show your work below.

CRITICAL THINKING

8. Evaluating Conclusions If there were no land on Earth's surface, what would the pattern of surface currents look like? Explain your answer.

____

____

____

____

9. Making Comparisons Compare the factors that contribute to the formation of surface currents and deep currents.

____

____

____

____

Section Review

Currents and Climate

USING KEY TERMS

1. Use each of the following terms in a separate sentence: *upwelling*, *El Niño*, and *La Niña*.

____

____

____

UNDERSTANDING KEY IDEAS

______ 2. The Gulf Stream carries warm water to the North Atlantic Ocean, which contributes to
   a. a harsh winter in the British Isles.
   b. a cold-water surface current that flows to the British Isles.
   c. a mild climate for the British Isles.
   d. a warm-water surface current that flows along the coast of California.

3. Why might the climate in Scotland be relatively mild even though the country is located at a high latitude?

____

____

4. Name two disasters caused by El Niño.

____

____

MATH SKILLS

5. A fisher usually catches 540 kg of anchovies off the coast of Peru. During El Niño, the fisher caught 85% less fish. How many kilograms of fish did the fisher catch during El Niño? Show your work below.

Section Review *continued*

CRITICAL THINKING

6. Applying Concepts Many marine organisms depend on upwelling to bring nutrients to the surface. How might El Niño affect a fisher's way of life?

____

____

____

____

Name _________________________________ Class _______________ Date _____________

Section Review

Waves

USING KEY TERMS

For each pair of terms, explain how the meanings of the terms differ.

1. *whitecap* and *swell*

____

____

2. *undertow* and *longshore current*

____

____

3. *tsunami* and *storm surge*

____

____

UNDERSTANDING KEY IDEAS

_______ **4.** Longshore currents transport sediment
    a. to the open ocean.   **c.** only during low tide.
    b. along the shore.   **d.** only during high tide.

5. Where do deep-water waves become shallow-water waves?

____

____

6. Explain how water moves as waves travel through it.

____

____

____

7. Name five events that can cause a tsunami.

____

____

____

____

Section Review *continued*

8. Describe the two parts of a wave.

____

____

MATH SKILLS

9. If a barrier island that is 1 km wide and 10 km long loses 1.5 m of its width per year to erosion by a longshore current, how long will the island take to lose one-fourth of its width? Show your work below.

CRITICAL THINKING

10. Analyzing Processes How would you explain a bottle moving across the water in the same direction that the waves are traveling? Make a drawing of the bottle's movement.

____

____

____

____

Section Review *continued*

11. Analyzing Processes Describe the motion of a wave as it approaches the shore.

____

____

____

12. Applying Concepts Explain how energy plays a role in the creation of ocean waves.

____

____

____

13. Making Comparisons How does the formation of an undertow differ from the formation of a longshore current? How is sand on the beach affected by each?

____

____

____

Section Review

Tides

USING KEY TERMS

1. In your own words, write a definition for each of the following terms: *spring tides* and *neap tides*.

____

____

UNDERSTANDING KEY IDEAS

______ 2. Tides are at their highest during
   - **a.** spring tide.
   - **b.** neap tide.
   - **c.** a tidal bore.
   - **d.** the daytime.

3. Which tides have minimum tidal range? Which tides have maximum tidal range?

____

____

____

4. What causes tidal ranges?

____

____

____

MATH SKILLS

5. If it takes 24 h and 50 min for a spot on Earth that is facing the moon to rotate to face the moon again, how many minutes does it take? Show your work below.

| Section Review *continued*

CRITICAL THINKING

6. Applying Concepts How many days pass between the minimum and the
maximum of the tidal range in any given area? Explain your answer.

____

____

____

____

7. Analyzing Processes Explain how the position of the moon relates to the
occurrence of high tides and low tides.

____

____

____

____

Chapter Review

USING KEY TERMS

For each pair of terms, explain how the meanings of the terms differ.

1. *surface current* and *deep current*

____

____

2. *El Niño* and *La Niña*

____

____

3. *spring tide* and *neap tide*

____

____

4. *tide* and *tidal range*

____

____

UNDERSTANDING KEY IDEAS

Multiple Choice

_______ **5.** Deep currents form when
   a. cold air decreases water density.
   b. warm air increases water density.
   c. the ocean surface freezes and solids from the water underneath are removed.
   d. salinity increases.

_______ **6.** When waves come near the shore,
   a. they speed up.
   b. they maintain their speed.
   c. their wavelength increases.
   d. their wave height increases.

_______ **7.** Whitecaps break
   a. in the surf.
   b. in the breaker zone.
   c. in the open ocean.
   d. as their wavelength increases.

_______ **8.** Tidal range is greatest during
   a. spring tide.
   b. neap tide.
   c. a tidal bore.
   d. the daytime.

Chapter Review *continued*

_______ **9.** Tides alternate between high and low because the moon revolves around the Earth
    a. at the same speed the Earth rotates.
    b. at a much faster speed than the Earth rotates.
    c. at a much slower speed than the Earth rotates.
    d. at different speeds.

_______ **10.** El Niño can cause
    a. droughts to occur in Indonesia and Australia.
    b. upwelling to occur off the coast of South America.
    c. earthquakes.
    d. droughts to occur in the southern half of the United States.

Short Answer

11. Explain the relationship between upwelling and El Niño.

____

____

12. Describe the two parts of a wave. Describe how these two parts relate to wavelength and wave height.

____

____

13. Compare the relative positions of the Earth, moon, and sun during the spring and neap tides.

____

____

14. Explain the difference between the breaker zone and the surf.

____

____

15. Describe how warm-water currents affect the climate in the British Isles.

____

____

16. Describe the factors that form deep currents.

____

____

Chapter Review *continued*

CRITICAL THINKING

17. Concept Mapping Use the following terms to create a concept map: *wind, deep currents, sun's gravity, types of ocean-water movement, surface currents, tides, increasing water density, waves,* and *moon's gravity.*

18. Identifying Relationships Why are tides more noticeable in Earth's oceans than on its land?

____

____

____

19. Expressing Opinions Explain why it's important to study El Niño and La Niña.

____

____

____

20. Applying Concepts Suppose you and a friend are planning a fishing trip to the ocean. Your friend tells you that the fish bite more in his secret fishing spot during low tide. If low tide occurred at the spot at 7 a.m. today and you are going to fish there in 1 week, at what time will low tide occur in that spot?

____

____

____

____

21. Identifying Relationships Describe how global winds, the Coriolis Effect, and continental deflections form a pattern of surface currents on Earth.

____

____

____

____

| Chapter Review *continued*

INTERPRETING GRAPHICS

The diagram below shows some of Earth's major surface currents that flow in the Western Hemisphere. Use the diagram to answer the questions that follow.

22. List two warm-water currents and two cold-water currents.

____

____

23. How do you think the Labrador Current affects the climate of Canada and Greenland?

____

____

Reinforcement

Going with the Flow

Complete this worksheet after you finish reading the section "Currents."

It's the adventure of a lifetime—a trip around the world, entirely under sail. Here's your chance to take on the global sailing challenge without even getting wet. Use this map to plan your adventure. Answer the questions as you plan your route.

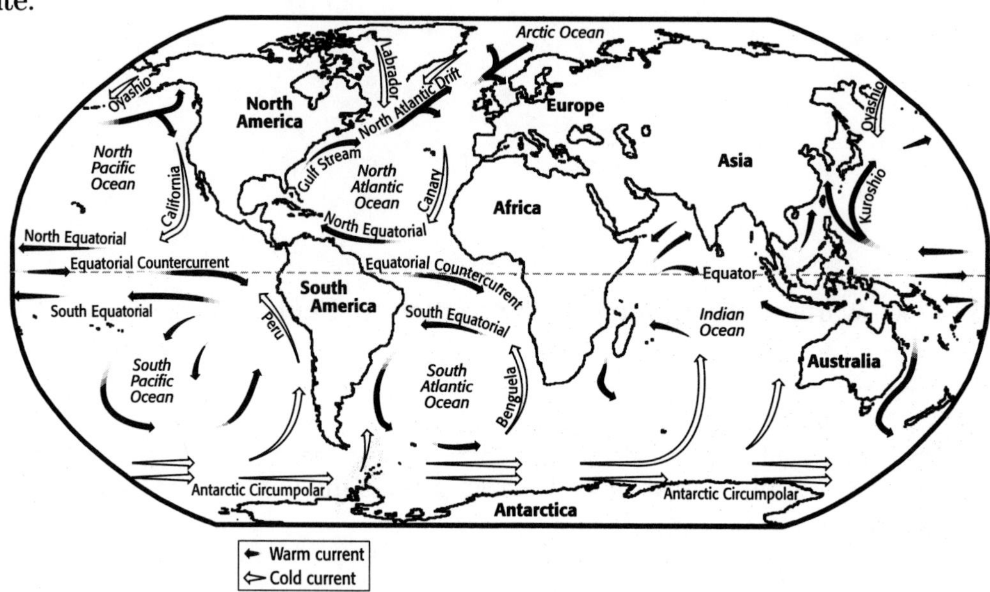

1. Choose the location from which you will set sail.

____

____

2. Which ocean current lies offshore from where you set sail?

____

____

3. If you float your boat on this current, where will it take you? List the currents whose flow will take you around the world. If the current is not named on the map, describe its direction.

____

____

____

____

Reinforcement *continued*

The following questions will help you identify possible trouble on your journey. Use the names of ocean currents in your answers.

4. Which currents flow in different directions from the currents you will be riding? Where are these currents near your currents?

____

____

____

5. Where are the currents deflected by continents or chains of islands?

____

____

____

6. Where do currents form large circles that might take you for an unnecessary spin?

____

____

____

7. Where do currents coming from the poles make the sailing unusually cold?

____

____

____

8. Revise your route based on your answers to questions 4 to 7. Then write a short paragraph describing the route of your sailing adventure.

____

____

____

Reinforcement

Mastering the Waves

Complete this worksheet after you finish reading the section "Waves."

After many weeks at sea, you've become a master at sailing on the open ocean. You are, of course, sharing your adventure with others by keeping a daily sailing record, or *log*. (Maybe your log is even online.)

Add the name of your boat to the title of this log. Write in the dates. Then use the terms listed below to fill in the blanks and complete the information.

breakers	crest	storm surges
surf	swell	trough
tsunamis	undertow	wave height
whitecaps		

Log for the Voyage of the _________________________________

1. Date: _________________________. This was a glorious day for sailing. The winds were steady. For the most part, the waves were only gentle, rolling

_________________________. However, for a few hours in the afternoon the wind became quite brisk, the waves picked up, and we were treated to the

sight of _________________________ splashing across the horizon.

2. Date: _________________________. The day began with no wind at all. But there were dark clouds on the horizon, so we prepared for bad weather. Sure enough, the wind picked up and the sea got rough. Soon we were on a roller

coaster ride. Down in the _________________________ of each wave, it seemed

as if we were walled in by water. Up at the _________________________, we could see that these walls of water stretched into the distance. After four more hours of pitching and rolling, we had a brief rain, and then the seas calmed down.

3. Date: _________________________. The seas were choppy today. From crest to

trough, the _________________________ was about 6 feet. Our decks were sprayed as we crested each wave. It rained just enough to give us much appreciated fresh water showers.

4. Date: _________________________. Today we ran into our first bad weather in a week and had some scary moments. The wind blew up very suddenly, and kept changing directions. We battled higher and higher waves. Then we saw

land ahead. We got close enough to see the rows of _________________________

Reinforcement *continued*

heading toward the shore. We were blown even closer, and we could see the white ribbon of the beach. I imagined our boat being driven into the

_________________________ and breaking to bits, and ourselves swept back out

to sea by the _________________________. The worst didn't happen. We managed to swing the sails around and catch a breeze that moved us back out to sea. But I knew then that I would never make a good surfer.

5. Date: _________________________. The radio reported a mild earthquake,

thousands of miles to the north of us, but still across the same ocean. So we

have kept the radio on for alerts of _________________________

6. Date: _________________________. After several rough days in a row, we were

all exhausted. We voted to change our route and head for a short land break at this delightful tropical port. After we landed we heard that a serious storm

had hit our original destinations, with _________________________ of several

feet flooding the whole area. So we feel pretty lucky that we decided to change our route.

Critical Thinking

Trouble in Waves

You're the captain of the cruise ship *Paradise Found*. Your ship is on the open ocean, halfway between Alaska and Hawaii, when you get the following announcement over the radio.

"The Pacific Tsunami Warning Center has just detected a massive underwater earthquake in the middle of the North Pacific. Waves with wavelengths of 100 km and wave heights of 2 m are traveling at 700 km/h. The waves are expected to hit the southwestern coast of Alaska within 2 hours. Stay tuned for further information."

UNDERSTANDING CONCEPTS

1. What happens to the size of waves as they approach the shore? Why does this happen?

____

____

____

____

2. What happens to the water in a wave after it crashes into the surf?

____

____

____

____

PREDICTING CONSEQUENCES

3. Which is in more danger, the cruise ship or the coastal areas? Explain your answer.

____

____

____

| Critical Thinking *continued*

4. What damage might be done to the coast of southwestern Alaska?

____

____

____

5. After the waves of the tsunami hit the land, what will happen to all that extra water?

____

____

____

6. Will the waves of the tsunami push the *Paradise Found* ashore? Why or why not?

____

____

____

DRAWING CONCLUSIONS

7. What should people in coastal areas do when there is a tsunami warning?

____

____

____

8. What should ships at sea do when there is a tsunami warning?

____

____

____

Section Quiz

Section: Currents

Write the letter of the correct answer in the space provided.

______ **1.** Two examples of surface currents are the Gulf Stream and the
- **a.** Brazil Current.
- **b.** Antarctic Bottom Water.
- **c.** Coriolis effect.
- **d.** North Atlantic Deep Water.

______ **2.** Surface currents are caused by
- **a.** floods.
- **b.** warm water.
- **c.** the wind.
- **d.** the equator.

______ **3.** Ocean currents flow from east to west near the
- **a.** Gulf Stream.
- **b.** poles.
- **c.** equator.
- **d.** global winds.

______ **4.** The curved paths of global winds and surface currents are caused by
- **a.** the rotation of the Earth.
- **b.** the Coriolis effect.
- **c.** warm air near the equator.
- **d.** continental deflection.

______ **5.** Ocean currents in the Northern and Southern Hemispheres turn
- **a.** from west to east.
- **b.** in opposite directions.
- **c.** clockwise.
- **d.** against the Earth's rotation.

______ **6.** What does a surface current do when it deflects?
- **a.** gains speed
- **b.** moves toward cold water
- **c.** meets another ocean current
- **d.** changes direction

______ **7.** The density of ocean water increases when it
- **a.** joins the Gulf Stream.
- **b.** gets colder.
- **c.** gets warmer.
- **d.** turns to ice.

______ **8.** Which process increases the salinity of ocean water?
- **a.** the Coriolis effect
- **b.** convection currents
- **c.** evaporation
- **d.** continental deflection

______ **9.** As water gets denser, how does it move?
- **a.** expands toward warmer water
- **b.** sinks toward the ocean floor
- **c.** gets pushed toward the poles
- **d.** gets pulled up by evaporation

______ **10.** Which currents carry warm water away from the equator?
- **a.** deep currents
- **b.** evaporation
- **c.** surface currents
- **d.** freezing

Section Quiz

Section: Currents and Climate

Match the correct description with the correct term. Write the letter in the space provided.

_______ **1.** type of current that creates warmer climates along a coastal area

_______ **2.** type of current that creates cooler climates in coastal areas

_______ **3.** where the Gulf Stream and other warm currents originate

_______ **4.** ocean current that warms the British Isles

_______ **5.** ocean current that cools the West Coast of the United States

_______ **6.** the movement of cold, nutrient-rich water to the surface of the ocean

_______ **7.** a change in the water temperature of the Pacific Ocean that produces a warm current

_______ **8.** a change in the water temperature of the eastern Pacific Ocean that produces cooler than usual surface water temperatures

_______ **9.** an unusually long period during which rainfall is below average

_______ **10.** used to collect data to predict an El Niño

a. California Current

b. cold-water

c. drought

d. El Niño

e. Gulf Stream

f. La Niña

g. buoys

h. Tropics

i. upwelling

j. warm-water

Name _______________________________ Class _____________ Date ____________

Section Quiz

Section: Waves

Write the letter of the correct answer in the space provided.

_______ **1.** The two main parts of a wave are the
- **a.** swell and whitecap.
- **b.** wavelength and wave height.
- **c.** crest and trough.
- **d.** rise and dip.

_______ **2.** As energy moves in waves through the water, the water moves
- **a.** in waves toward shore.
- **b.** in a small vertical circle.
- **c.** in the direction of the waves.
- **d.** against the current.

_______ **3.** When deep-water waves reach water shallower than one-half of their wavelength, they
- **a.** reverse their flow.
- **b.** enter the breaker zone.
- **c.** decrease in height.
- **d.** increase in height.

_______ **4.** What causes breakers to crash into the ocean floor?
- **a.** deep-water waves
- **b.** gravity
- **c.** short wavelengths
- **d.** shore currents

_______ **5.** Where does an undertow take sand and other particles from the shore?
- **a.** higher up on the shore
- **b.** as far as the first breaker
- **c.** out to sea
- **d.** farther on down the shore

_______ **6.** What transports most of the sediment in beach environments?
- **a.** undertows
- **b.** breakers
- **c.** longshore currents
- **d.** wind

_______ **7.** In the open ocean, whitecaps often form
- **a.** in places close to the shore.
- **b.** during storms.
- **c.** in warm-water currents.
- **d.** after swells go by.

_______ **8.** Which type of wave makes for the best sailing on the ocean?
- **a.** whitecaps
- **b.** tsunamis
- **c.** breakers
- **d.** swells

_______ **9.** A tsunami occurs when a large volume of water suddenly
- **a.** moves up and down.
- **b.** forms a giant wave.
- **c.** gets sucked below the surface.
- **d.** turns hotter or colder.

_______ **10.** What are the most destructive parts of hurricanes?
- **a.** tsunamis
- **b.** winds
- **c.** storm surges
- **d.** breakers

Section Quiz

Section: Tides

Match the correct description with the correct term. Write the letter in the space provided.

_______ **1.** the periodic daily rise and fall of ocean water

_______ **2.** the force that pulls the tides

_______ **3.** main source of gravity for tides

_______ **4.** bulge that takes place on parts of Earth facing or opposite the moon

_______ **5.** forms when water is drawn away from the area between high tides

_______ **6.** celestial body around which Earth rotates

_______ **7.** the difference between water levels at low and high tide

_______ **8.** tides that occur during the new and full moons

_______ **9.** tides that occur during the first and third quarters of the moon

_______ **10.** a body of water that rushes into a narrow bay and causes a very sudden tidal rise

a. gravity

b. high tide

c. low tide

d. moon

e. neap tide

f. spring tide

g. sun

h. tidal bore

i. tidal range

j. tides

Chapter Test A

The Movement of Ocean Water
MULTIPLE CHOICE
Write the letter of the correct answer in the space provided.

_______ **1.** In 1947 Thor Heyerdahl sailed a simple raft from Peru to Polynesia, following the ocean currents for more than 6,000 kilometers. Which statement accurately describes what Heyerdahl proved by this voyage?
  a. Ancient Peru was settled by people from Polynesia.
  b. People from ancient Peru were the first settlers of Polynesia.
  c. It would have been possible for people from ancient Peru to reach Polynesia by following ocean currents.
  d. Polynesia was settled accidentally when rafts from Peru were carried out by ocean currents.

_______ **2.** Surface ocean currents such as the Gulf Stream
  a. move warm water from higher latitudes to lower latitudes.
  b. transport many times more water than all the rivers in the world.
  c. are formed in parts of the ocean where water density is great.
  d. move in straight paths across the oceans.

_______ **3.** In which direction do global winds blow ocean currents near the equator?
  a. from east to west   **c.** counterclockwise
  b. from west to east   **d.** away from the poles

_______ **4.** Trying to roll a ball straight across a turning merry-go-round is a demonstration of what happens in the
  a. movement of global winds across the surface of the ocean.
  b. flow of currents and countercurrents at the equator.
  c. Coriolis effect.
  d. deflection of a current against a continent.

_______ **5.** Which surface current is deflected by the continent of South America?
  a. California Current   **c.** Brazil Current
  b. Labrador Current   **d.** North Equatorial Current

_______ **6.** Compared with surface currents, deep currents are
  a. colder and less dense.   **c.** warmer and denser.
  b. warmer and less dense.   **d.** colder and denser.

| Chapter Test A *continued*

_______ **7.** When the air above water gets cold, what happens to water molecules?
   a. The water molecules evaporate, decreasing the water's density.
   b. The molecules slow down and move closer together, increasing the water's density.
   c. The water's volume increases as molecules move closer together.
   d. The denser water floats on top of the chilled water.

_______ **8.** Which of the following causes water from deep currents to rise to the surface to replace warm currents?
   a. the flow of warm currents from the equator toward the poles
   b. freezing of the surface of the water
   c. increased salinity due to evaporation
   d. squeezing solids out of the ice down into the water below

_______ **9.** How do warm-water currents affect the coastal areas along which they flow?
   a. They create greater rainfall along the coast.
   b. They create unusually cool climates for the latitude.
   c. They create unusually warm climates for the latitude.
   d. They make the coastal climate cooler than the inland climate.

_______ **10.** Which statement describes the negative effects of El Niño?
   a. El Niño appears every 2 to 12 years.
   b. Rain, flash floods, and mudslides occur in places where there is usually little rain, while usually wet areas suffer from drought.
   c. Sometimes El Niño is followed by La Niña, during which ocean temperatures become cooler.
   d. Upwelling along the coast of South America occurs after an El Niño.

_______ **11.** It is important for scientists to learn as much as possible about El Niño because the weather pattern
   a. has so far been completely unpredictable.
   b. affects North America more than any other continent.
   c. has so many effects on organisms and land.
   d. can only be studied out in the open ocean.

MATCHING

Match the correct definition with the correct term. Write the letter in the space provided. Some terms will not be used.

_______ **12.** the lowest part of a wave

_______ **13.** the highest part of a wave

_______ **14.** the vertical distance between the highest and lowest points of a wave

_______ **15.** the vertical difference between two adjacent high points or two adjacent low points of a wave

a. crest

b. current

c. swell

d. trough

e. wavelength

f. wave height

MULTIPLE CHOICE

Write the letter of the correct answer in the space provided.

_______ **16.** How do you calculate wave speed?
  a. Divide the wave period by the wavelength.
  b. Divide the wavelength by the wave period.
  c. Divide the wave height by the wave period.
  d. Multiply the wavelength by the wave height.

_______ **17.** Why do waves increase in height as they approach the shore?
  a. The waves are forced into narrow inlets of land.
  b. The water particles speed up as they approach land.
  c. The water's density decreases because it's warmer near the shore.
  d. The waves begin to interact with the ocean floor.

_______ **18.** In what direction does an undertow flow?
  a. in the same direction of the wave
  b. at right angles to the wave
  c. in the opposite direction as the wave
  d. parallel to the wave

_______ **19.** An earthquake causes a tsunami because force from the quake
  a. pushes a large body of water up from the ocean floor.
  b. pulls water down toward the source of the quake.
  c. blows surface water away from the shore.
  d. meets the force of currents flowing in a different direction.

_______ **20.** Which statement describes what is happening at high tide?
  a. The moon is revolving more quickly than the Earth is rotating.
  b. The moon's gravity is dragging water away from the equator.
  c. The moon's gravity is pulling ocean water into a bulge.
  d. The sun's gravity pulls with more force than the moon's gravity.

Chapter Test A *continued*

_______**21.** Which statement explains why the moon's gravity is able to create high and low tides?
  a. The moon is revolving more quickly than the Earth is rotating.
  b. The moon is revolving more slowly than the Earth is rotating.
  c. Some parts of the Earth never face directly on the sun and moon.
  d. The moon is revolving at the same speed that the Earth is rotating.

_______**22.** Spring tides and neap tides occur in patterns governed by
  a. changes in the force of the Earth's gravity.
  b. the type of ocean currents near where the tides occur.
  c. whether the gravity of the sun or moon exerts a stronger pull.
  d. the relative positions of the Earth, moon, and sun (the phases of the moon).

_______**23.** From what is known about spring tides and neap tides, you can conclude that
  a. the sun's gravity exerts the most power when the moon is on the opposite side of the Earth from the sun.
  b. the height of high tides varies with the phases of the moon.
  c. spring tides and neap tides affect the phases of the moon.
  d. the moon revolves around the Earth every 14 days.

_______**24.** A tidal bore is most likely to occur along a coast that has
  a. lower than usual tidal ranges.
  b. both warm- and cold-water currents offshore.
  c. narrow bays, inlets, and river channels.
  d. landforms that deflect the currents.

Chapter Test B

The Movement of Ocean Water

USING KEY TERMS

Use the terms from the following list to complete the sentences below. Each term may be used only once. Some terms may not be used.

Coriolis effect	deep currents	El Niño
surface currents	tides	tidal range
tsunami	upwelling	wavelength

1. Although they flow near the top of the ocean, _______________________ can reach depths of several hundred meters.

2. Although they flow near the bottom of the ocean, _______________________ sometimes flow on top of other currents.

3. The negative effects of _______________________ include flash floods, mudslides and droughts.

4. The _______________________ is used to measure wave periods and therefore wave speed.

5. The difference between levels of ocean water at high tide and low tide is called a(n) _______________________.

UNDERSTANDING KEY IDEAS

Write the letter of the correct answer in the space provided.

______ **6.** How do changes in the circulation of ocean currents affect climate?
    a. by changing the atmosphere   **c.** by increasing salinity
    b. by moving water clockwise   **d.** by changing the tides

______ **7.** Which event does NOT happen as the result of an upwelling?
    a. Cold-water currents replace warm-water currents.
    b. Surface currents flow away from the shore.
    c. The California Current moves water south from the North Pacific.
    d. Plants get the minerals they need for photosynthesis.

______ **8.** If the wavelength of a wave stays the same, what happens when the wave period increases?
    a. increase in wave speed   **c.** decrease in wave speed
    b. increase in wave height   **d.** decrease in wave height

Chapter Test B *continued*

_______ **9.** Which of the following is most likely to spread pollution along the shore?
    a. upwelling   **c.** undertow
    b. breaker   **d.** longshore current

_______ **10.** When do the greatest tidal ranges occur?
    a. spring tides   **c.** high tides
    b. neap tides   **d.** low tides

11. What three factors control surface currents?

____

____

____

12. What are three factors that control deep currents?

____

____

____

13. What forms of technology are scientists using to study El Niño?

____

____

____

14. Explain why waves break as they reach the shore.

____

____

____

15. Explain how the positions of the Earth, moon, and sun affect the tides.

____

____

____

____

CRITICAL THINKING

16. Do winds and currents flow faster at the equator than at the poles, or more slowly? Think about what you know regarding the shape and rotation of the Earth, the directions of currents, and convection. Make inferences from what you know. Then give reasons to support your answer.

____

____

____

____

17. El Niño can prevent upwelling along the Pacific Coast. What might happen if normal upwelling does not take place? Make predictions and support them with facts from the chapter.

____

____

____

____

18. How might a heavy undertow affect the formation of breakers above it? Use your answer to question 14 to form a hypothesis.

____

____

____

____

19. Why should people who live in coastal areas learn about currents, waves, and tides? Give examples of how waves and tides could affect everyday lives.

____

____

____

____

| Chapter Test B *continued*

CONCEPT MAPPING

20. Use the following terms to complete the concept map below:

breakers deep-water waves surf
swells undertow

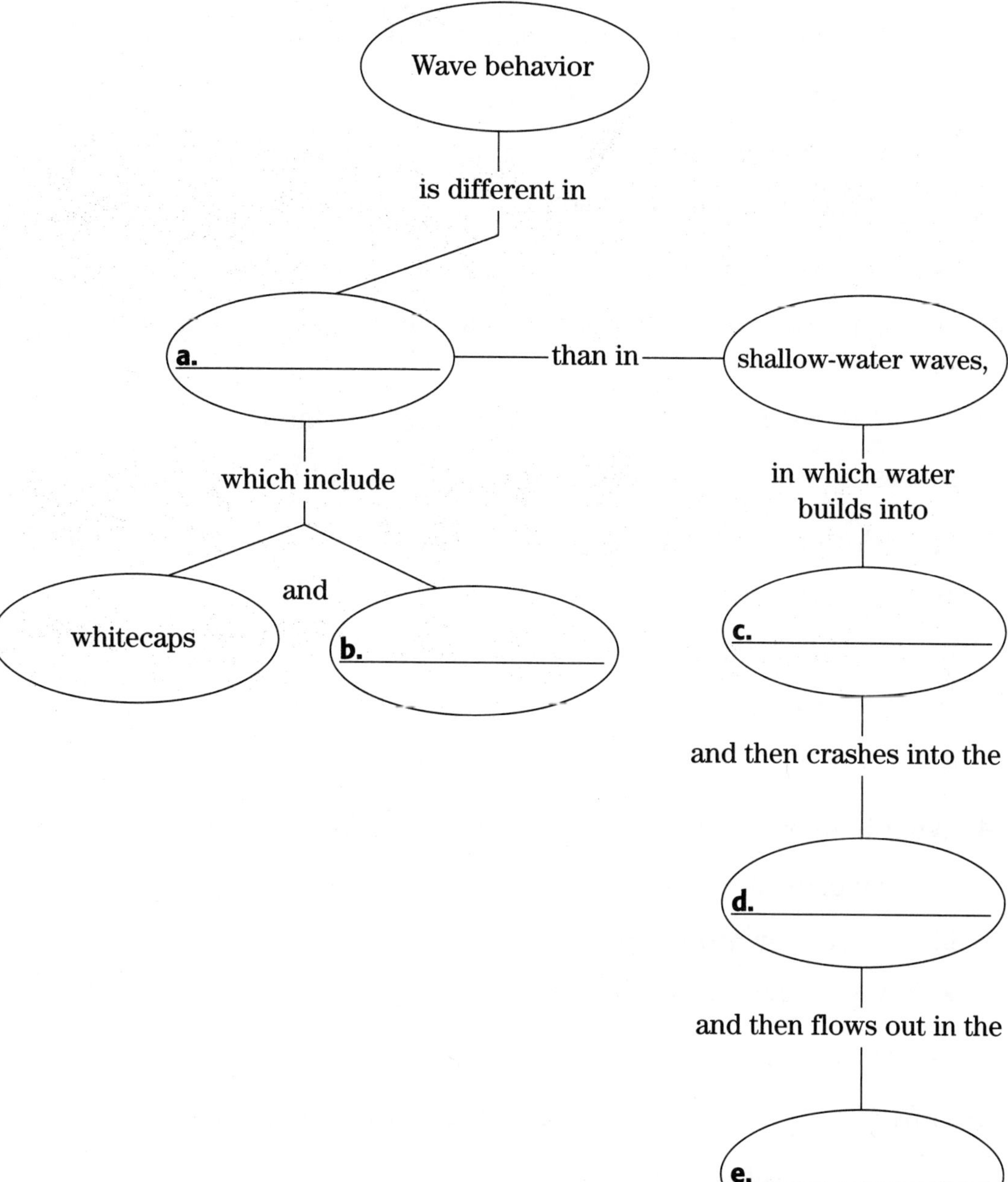

Chapter Test C

THE MOVEMENT OF OCEAN WATER
MULTIPLE CHOICE
Circle the letter of the best answer for each question.

1. Which phrase describes a surface current?

   a. gets cool near the equator

   b. flows like a stream

   c. stretches from north to south

   d. creates global winds

2. In what direction do global winds and currents flow near the equator?

   a. east to west   **c.** toward the land

   b. west to east   **d.** north to south

3. How does the Coriolis effect make ocean currents appear to move?

   a. back and forth

   b. in a curved path

   c. clockwise

   d. against the Earth's rotation

4. What happens to an ocean current when it hits a continent?

   a. It changes direction.

   b. It moves toward the poles.

   c. It moves toward the equator.

   d. It speeds up.

5. How are deep currents different from surface currents?

   a. They are warmer and faster.

   b. They are caused by winds.

   c. They are denser and slower.

   d. Some are colder than others.

Circle the letter of the best answer for each question.

6. What happens to water when the air above it gets cold?

   a. It evaporates.

   b. It slows down and cools.

   c. It moves faster to stay warm.

   d. Its salinity increases.

7. What happens to the water that is left behind after evaporation?

   a. It gets hotter.

   b. It gets less dense.

   c. It moves faster to stay warm.

   d. Its salinity increases.

8. What is the highest point of a wave?

   a. crest

   b. trough

   c. wave height

   d. wavelength

9. What is the lowest point of a wave?

   a. crest

   b. trough

   c. wave height

   d. wavelength

10. What is the distance between two crests or troughs?

   a. crest   **c.** wave height

   b. trough   **d.** wavelength

11. What is the vertical distance between a crest and a trough?

   a. crest   **c.** wave height

   b. trough   **d.** wavelength

| Chapter Test C *continued*

MATCHING

Read the description. Then, <u>draw a line</u> from the dot next to each description to the matching word.

12. current that flows south to cool the West Coast of the United States ●

13. a long-term weather pattern that can be changed by an ocean current ●

14. current that carries water from the Tropics to the British Isles ●

15. a rise of cold water from deep in the ocean to the warmer surface ●

a. California Current

b. climate

c. Gulf Stream

d. upwelling

---

16. weather pattern that makes the ocean surface cooler ●

17. weather pattern that makes the ocean surface warmer ●

18. devices used to collect data to predict an El Niño ●

19. a long period of time with no rain ●

a. drought

b. El Niño

c. La Niña

d. buoys

| Chapter Test C *continued*

FILL-IN-THE-BLANK

Read the words in the box. Read the sentences. <u>Fill in each blank</u> with the word or phrase that best completes the sentence.

breakers	tides	moon
tsunamis	tidal bore	wave period

20. A measurement of the time between two waves is called a

_____________________.

21. Waves that build up and then crash into the ocean floor are known

as _____________________.

22. Huge waves called _____________________ are caused by

underwater earthquakes, volcanic eruptions, and landslides.

23. The most important force that creates tides is the gravity of the

_____________________.

24. Neap, spring, high, and low are all types of

_____________________.

25. A narrow inlet of land along a coast is where you might see a

_____________________. This causes a very sudden rise in

the tide.

Assessment

Performance-Based Assessment

OBJECTIVES

In this activity you will demonstrate the Coriolis effect and discuss how it affects ocean currents.

KNOW THE SCORE!

As you work through the activity, keep in mind that you will be earning a grade for the following.

- how well you work with the materials and equipment (30%)
- the quality and clarity of your observations (40%)
- how well you analyze the Coriolis effect in relationship to the Earth's axis and rotation (30%)

Using Scientific Methods

ASK QUESTIONS

In what directions does the Coriolis effect take place?

How does the Coriolis effect influence ocean currents?

MATERIALS AND EQUIPMENT

- one-quarter sheet of poster board
- full sheet of foam board larger than the poster board
- crayon or marker
- pushpin

- scissors
- a marble
- a partner to help you make and record your observations

SAFETY INFORMATION 

- Instruct students on basic safety with scissors and pointed objects such as pushpins.
- Do not eat or drink anything in the laboratory.

MAKE AND OBSERVE A MODEL

1. Write the letter N (for North) in the center of the poster board. In the center of the other side, write the letter S (for South). Hold the board and rotate it counterclockwise, with the N side facing up. Have your partner sit or kneel under the board and observe the S. In what direction is the S rotating, compared to the N?

____

____

| Performance-Based Assessment *continued*

---

2. Make a hole large enough for your finger near one edge of the poster board. Use the tip of a closed pair of scissors to enlarge the hole. Push the pushpin through the center of the board and into the foam board.

3. Put your finger in the finger hole and slowly rotate the board counterclockwise. Have your partner roll the marble across the board, making sure the marble doesn't hit your finger. Describe the path the marble takes.

---

4. While still rotating the board counterclockwise, try rolling the marble in a few different directions. Describe what happens.

FORM A HYPOTHESIS

5. What will happen if you rotate the board counterclockwise?

TEST THE HYPOTHESIS

6. Rotate the board clockwise. Which pole does the center of the board now represent?

---

7. While you rotate the board clockwise, have your partner roll the marble again, from different directions. Describe the path the marble takes.

DRAW CONCLUSIONS

8. Relate what you have observed in this activity to ocean currents.

Standardized Test Preparation

READING

Read each of the passages below. Then, answer the questions that follow each passage.

Passage 1 When certain algae grow rapidly, they clump together on the ocean's surface in an algal bloom that changes the color of the water. Because these algal blooms often turn the water red or reddish brown and tidal conditions were believed to cause the blooms, people called these blooms *red tides*. However, algal blooms are not always red and are not directly related to tides. Scientists now call these algae clusters <u>harmful algal blooms (HABs)</u>. HABs are considered harmful because the species of algae that makes up the blooms produces toxins that can poison fish and shellfish, which in turn can poison people.

Unfortunately, seafood contamination is not noticeable without testing and is not easily eliminated. The toxins don't change the flavor of the seafood, and cooking the seafood doesn't eliminate the toxins.

_______ **1.** Why did scientists start calling red tides *HABs*?
   A The name *HABs* is easier to remember.
   B The name *red tides* was not accurate in describing the phenomenon.
   C The algal blooms are actually green.
   D The term *red tides* did not reflect the danger of the blooms.

_______ **2.** How can a person tell if seafood has been contaminated by HABs?
   F Contaminated seafood has a reddish color.
   G HABs change the flavor of the seafood.
   H Seafood contaminated by HABs has a strange smell.
   I Unfortunately, there is no easy way to tell.

Standardized Test Preparation *continued*

Passage 2 Tsunamis are the most destructive waves in the ocean. Most tsunamis are caused by earthquakes on the ocean floor, but some can be caused by volcanic eruptions and underwater landslides. Tsunamis are sometimes called *tidal waves*, which is <u>misleading</u> because tsunamis have no connection with tides.

Tsunamis commonly have a wave period of about 15 min and a wave speed of about 725 km/h, which is about as fast as a jet airliner. By the time a tsunami reaches the shore, its height may be 30 to 40 m.

In 1960, a tsunami was triggered by an earthquake off the coast of South America. The tsunami was so powerful that it crossed the Pacific Ocean and hit the city of Hilo, on the coast of Hawaii, approximately 10,000 km away. The same tsunami then continued on to strike Japan.

_______ **1.** The word *misleading* was used in this passage to describe the use of the term *tidal waves* because

  A tsunamis are related to tides.

  B tsunamis can cause extensive damage to shores.

  C tsunamis are related to earthquakes.

  D tsunamis are not related to tides.

_______ **2.** Which of the following statements is a fact from the passage?

  F All tsunamis are caused by earthquakes.

  G A tsunami can travel as fast as a jet airliner.

  H The tsunami of 1960 caused destruction only in Japan.

  I Tsunamis are caused by surface currents.

Standardized Test Preparation *continued*

INTERPRETING GRAPHICS

The diagram below shows the possible positions of the moon relative to the earth and sun during different tidal ranges. use the diagram below to answer the questions that follow.

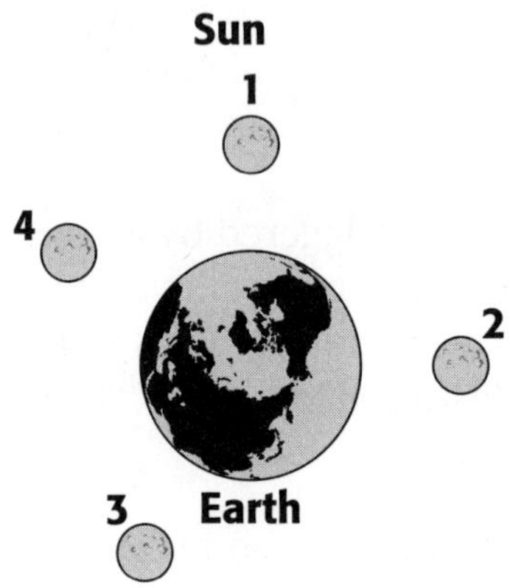

_______ **1.** At which position would the moon be during a neap tide?
    A 1
    B 2
    C 3
    D 4

_______ **2.** At which position would the moon be during a spring tide?
    F 1
    G 2
    H 3
    I 4

_______ **3.** The tidal range would be greater when the moon is at position 3 than when the moon is at position 4 because
    A position 4 forms a 90° angle with the sun and the Earth.
    B position 3 is very near a neap-tide position.
    C position 3 is very near a spring-tide position.
    D position 4 is very near a spring-tide position.

Standardized Test Preparation *continued*

MATH

Read each answer below, and choose the best answer.

_______ **1.** If a wave has a speed of 3 m/s and a wavelength of 12 m, what is its period? Use the following equation to answer the question above:

$$\frac{\text{wavelength (m)}}{\text{wave period (s)}} = \text{wave speed (m/s)}$$

    A 36 s
    B 4 m
    C 24 s
    D 4 s

_______ **2.** Antarctic Bottom Water takes 750 years to move from the Antarctic coast to the equator. If the distance between the equator and the Antarctic coast is about 10,000 km, approximately how many kilometers does the bottom water move each year?
    F 13 km
    G 200 km
    H 75 km
    I 1 km

_______ **3.** A boat is traveling north at 20 km/h against a current that is moving south at 12 km/h. What is the overall speed and direction of the boat?
    A 8 km/h north
    B 8 km/h south
    C 32 km/h north
    D 32 km/h south

_______ **4.** Imagine that you are in a rowboat on the open ocean. You count 2 waves traveling right under your boat in 10 seconds. You estimate the wavelength to be 3 m. What is the wave speed?
    F 0.6 m/s
    G 6.0 m/s
    H 0.3 m/s
    I 3.0 m/s

DATASHEET FOR CHAPTER LAB

Up from the Depths

Every year, the water in certain parts of the ocean "turns over." That is, the water at the bottom rises to the top and the water at the top falls to the bottom. This yearly change brings fresh nutrients from the bottom of the ocean to the fish living near the surface. However, the water in some parts of the ocean never turns over. By completing this activity, you will find out why not.

Keep in mind that some parts of the ocean are warmer at the bottom, and some are warmer at the top. And sometimes the saltiest water is at the bottom and sometimes not. As you complete this activity, you will investigate how these factors help determine whether the water will turn over.

OBJECTIVES

Demonstrate the effects of temperature and salinity on the density of water.

Describe why some parts of the ocean turn over, while others do not.

MATERIALS

- beakers, 400 mL (5)
- blue and red food coloring
- bucket of ice
- gloves, heat-resistant
- plastic wrap, 4 pieces, approximately 30.cm × 20 cm
- hot plate
- salt
- spoon
- tap water
- watch or clock

SAFETY INFORMATION 

Using Scientific Methods

ASK A QUESTION

1. Why do some parts of the ocean turn over and not others?

____

____

FORM A HYPOTHESIS

2. Write a hypothesis that is a possible answer to the question above. Explain your reasoning.

____

____

____

Up from the Depths *continued*

TEST THE HYPOTHESIS

3. Label the beakers 1 through 5. Fill beakers 1 through 4 with tap water.

4. Add a drop of blue food coloring to the water in beakers 1 and 2, and stir with the spoon.

5. Place beaker 1 in the bucket of ice for 10 min.

6. Add a drop of red food coloring to the water in beakers 3 and 4, and stir with the spoon.

7. Set beaker 3 on a hot plate turned to a low setting for 10 min.

8. Add one spoonful of salt to the water in beaker 4, and stir with the spoon.

9. While beaker 1 is cooling and beaker 3 is heating, copy the observations table below on a sheet of paper.

Observations Table	
Mixture of water	**Observations**
Warm water placed above cold water	
Cold water placed above warm water	
Salty water placed above fresh water	
Fresh water placed above salty water	

10. Pour half of the water in beaker 1 into beaker 5. Return beaker 1 to the bucket of ice.

11. Tuck a sheet of plastic wrap into beaker 5 so that the plastic rests on the surface of the water and lines the upper half of the beaker.

12. Put on your gloves. Slowly pour half of the water in beaker 3 into the plastic-lined upper half of beaker 5 to form two layers of water. Return beaker 3 to the hot plate, and remove your gloves.

13. Very carefully, pull on one edge of the plastic wrap and remove it so that the warm, red water rests on the cold, blue water.

Caution: The plastic wrap may be warm.

14. Wait about 5 minutes, and then observe the layers in beaker 5. Did one layer remain on top of the other? Was there any mixing or turning over? Record your observations in your observations table.

____

____

15. Empty beaker 5, and rinse it with clean tap water.

16. Repeat the procedure used in steps 10–15. This time, pour warm, red water from beaker 3 on the bottom and cold, blue water from beaker 1 on top. (Use gloves when pouring warm water.)

____

____

17. Again, repeat the procedure used in steps 10–15. This time, pour blue tap water from beaker 2 on the bottom and red, salty water from beaker 4 on top.

____

____

18. Repeat the procedure used in steps 10–15 a third time. This time, pour red, salty water from beaker 4 on the bottom and blue tap water from beaker 2 on top.

____

____

ANALYZE THE RESULTS

1. Analyzing Data Compare the results of all four trials. Explain why the water turned over in some of the trials but not in all of them.

____

____

____

____

____

DRAW CONCLUSIONS

2. Evaluating Results What is the effect of temperature and salinity on the density of water?

____

____

____

Up from the Depths *continued*

3. Drawing Conclusions What makes the temperature of ocean water decrease? What could make the salinity of ocean water increase?

____

____

____

____

4. Drawing Conclusions What reasons can you give to explain why some parts of the ocean do not turn over in the spring while some do?

____

____

____

APPLYING YOUR DATA

Suggest a method for setting up a model that tests the combined effects of temperature and salinity on the density of water. Consider using more than two water samples and dyes.

____

____

____

____

____

Quick Lab   **DATASHEET FOR QUICK LAB**

Doing the Wave

1. Tie one end of a **thin piece of rope** to a **doorknob**.

2. Tie a **ribbon** around the rope halfway between the doorknob and the other end of the rope.

3. Holding the rope at the untied end, quickly move the rope up and down and observe the ribbon.

4. How does the movement of the rope and ribbon relate to the movement of water and deep-water waves?

____

____

____

____

5. Repeat step 3, but move the rope higher and lower this time.

6. How does this affect the waves in the rope?

____

____

Model-Making Lab

Turning the Tides

Daily tides are caused by two "bulges" on the ocean's surface—one on the side of the Earth facing the moon and the other on the opposite side of the Earth. The bulge on the side facing the moon is caused by the moon's gravitational pull on the water. But the bulge on the opposite side of the Earth is slightly more difficult to explain. Whereas the moon pulls the water on one side of the Earth, the combined rotation of the Earth and the moon "pushes" the water on the opposite side of the Earth. In this activity, you will model the motion of the Earth and the moon to investigate the tidal bulge on the side of Earth facing away from the moon.

MATERIALS

- cardboard, 1 cm × 1 cm piece
- corrugated cardboard, one large and one small, with centers marked (2 disks)
- dowel, 1/4 in. in diameter and 36 cm long
- glue, white
- pencil, sharp
- stapler with staples
- string, 5 cm length

SAFETY INFORMATION 

PROCEDURE

1. Draw a line from the center of each disk along the folds in the cardboard to the edge of the disk. This line is the radius.

2. Place a drop of white glue on one end of the dowel. Lay the larger disk flat, and align the dowel with the line for the radius you drew in step 1. Insert about 2.5 cm of the dowel into the edge of the disk.

3. Add a drop of glue to the other end of the dowel, and push that end into the smaller disk, again along its radius. The setup should look like a large, two-headed lollipop. This setup is a model of the Earth-moon system.

4. Staple the string to the edge of the large disk on the side opposite the dowel. Staple the cardboard square to the other end of the string. This smaller piece of cardboard represents the Earth's oceans that face away from the moon.

5. Place the tip of the pencil at the center of the large disk and spin the model. You may poke a small hole in the bottom of the disk with your pencil, but DO NOT poke all the way through the cardboard. Record your observations. **Caution:** Be sure you are at a safe distance from other people before spinning your model.

|Turning the Tides *continued*

6. Now, find your model's center of mass. The center of mass is the point at which the model can be balanced on the end of the pencil. (Hint: It might be easier to find the center of mass by using the eraser end. Then, use the sharpened end of the pencil to balance the model.) This balance point should be just inside the edge of the larger disk.

7. Place the pencil at the center of mass, and spin the model around the pencil. Again, you may wish to poke a small hole in the disk. Record your observations.

ANALYZE THE RESULTS

1. What happened when you tried to spin the model around the center of the large disk? This model, called the Earth-centered model, represents the incorrect view that the moon orbits the center of the Earth.

____

____

____

2. What happened when you tried to spin the model around its center of mass? This point, called the barycenter, is the point around which both the Earth and the moon rotate.

____

____

____

____

3. In each case, what happened to the string and cardboard square when the model was spun?

____

____

____

____

____

| Turning the Tides *continued*

DRAW CONCLUSIONS

4. Which model—the Earth-centered model or the barycentric model—explains
why the Earth has a tidal bulge on the side opposite the moon? Explain your
answer.

____

____

____

____

____

____

Vocabulary Activity

Hidden Words About Ocean Water

After you finish reading the chapter, try this puzzle. Find 40 key words or terms from the chapter using the word list below. Read across and down on the grid. Circle the words as you find them.

O	C	E	A	N	S	C	U	R	R	E	N	T	S	S
N	O	A	A	W	A	V	E	L	E	N	G	T	H	U
P	R	S	W	W	L	O	N	G	S	H	O	R	E	N
A	I	T	A	H	I	N	D	E	N	S	I	T	Y	S
C	O	N	T	I	N	E	N	T	A	L	D	E	E	P
I	L	B	E	T	T	A	U	P	O	L	E	S	C	R
F	I	R	R	E	Y	P	P	S	U	R	F	U	R	I
I	S	E	D	C	P	T	W	W	N	T	L	R	E	N
C	E	A	R	A	E	I	E	T	D	S	E	F	S	G
S	F	K	O	P	R	D	L	R	E	U	C	A	T	E
W	F	E	U	S	I	E	L	O	R	N	T	C	R	L
E	E	R	G	T	O	J	I	U	T	A	I	E	A	N
L	C	S	H	O	D	J	N	G	O	M	O	O	N	I
L	T	C	T	R	H	I	G	H	W	I	N	D	G	Ñ
S	L	O	W	M	S	U	R	G	E	B	O	R	E	O

WORD LIST

bore	east	period	swells
breakers	El Niño	poles	tide
continental	high	range	trough
Coriolis effect	longshore	salinity	tsunami
crest	low	spring	undertow
currents	moon	storm	upwelling
deep	neap	sun	water
deflection	NOAA	surf	wavelength
density	ocean	surface	whitecaps
drought	Pacific	surge	wind

SciLinks Activity

CURRENTS

Go to www.scilinks.com. To find links related to ocean currents, type in the keyword HSM1061. Then use the links to answer the following questions about oceans and ocean currents.

SCiLINKS®

NSTA
Developed and maintained by the
National Science Teachers Association

Go to www.scilinks.org

Topic: Ocean Currents
SciLinks code: HSM1061

1. List at least five ocean currents.

____

____

____

2. What are the two largest ocean currents?

____

____

3. List at least five ocean habitats.

____

____

____

4. How does pressure change the density of ocean water?

____

____

5. What creates winds in the atmosphere and therefore currents in the ocean?

____

____

6. In general, how do temperatures of coastal areas compare to temperatures of inland areas nearby?

____

____

Performance-Based Assessment

Teacher Notes and Answer Key

PURPOSE

Students will demonstrate the Coriolis effect and observe it from both Northern and Southern Hemisphere orientations. They will then use their knowledge of the Earth's axis and rotation to explain ocean currents.

TIME REQUIRED

One 45-minute class period. Students will need 25 minutes to make and observe the model and 20 minutes to answer the analysis question.

RATINGS

Easy ← 1   2   3   4 → Hard

Teacher Prep–1
Student Set-Up–3
Concept Level–2
Clean Up–1

ADVANCE PREPARATION

Assemble the necessary materials (for each activity station): one-quarter sheet of poster board, a full sheet of foam board, a crayon or marker, a pushpin, scissors, and a marble. A globe helps students make the connection between the rotation of the poster board and the rotation of the Earth.

SAFETY INFORMATION

Instruct students on basic safety with scissors and pointed objects such as pushpins.

TEACHING STRATEGIES

To save both time and money, divide the class into three or four teams and have each team construct one model. Teams can then divide further into pairs and take turns doing the activity.

As students roll the marbles and watch them move across the rotating boards, encourage them to speculate on why the marble moves in a direction opposite to the rotation. Lead students to reason that the force of the rotation throws the marble forward.

• Rotate a globe as you discuss the Earth's rotation. Have students review the diagram of a globe in the "Currents" section as an aid to explain ocean currents.

Performance-Based Assessment *continued*

Evaluation Strategies

Use the following rubric to help evaluate student performance.

Rubric for Assessment

Possible points	Appropriate use of materials and equipment (30 points possible)
30–20	Successfully completes activity; safe and careful handling of materials and equipment; good attention to detail; superior lab skills
19–10	Generally completes activity; successful use of materials and equipment; moderate attention to detail
9–1	Does not complete activity; no attention to detail; apparent lack of skill
	Quality and clarity of observations (40 points possible)
40–30	Superior observations stated clearly and accurately; high level of detail
29–20	Accurate observations; moderate level of detail
19–10	Complete observations, but expressed in unclear manner; low level of detail
9–1	Erroneous, incomplete, or unclear observations; lack of details
	Explanation of observations (30 points possible)
30–20	Clear, detailed explanations; superior knowledge of the Coriolis effect; use of examples to support explanations
19–10	Less detailed explanation; adequate understanding of the Coriolis effect; some difficulty in expression
9–1	Vague explanations; poor understanding of the Coriolis effect; explanations unclear or not relevant; substantial factual errors

Name _____________________________ Class _______________ Date ___________

MODEL-MAKING

Performance-Based Assessment

OBJECTIVES

In this activity you will demonstrate the Coriolis effect and discuss how it affects ocean currents.

KNOW THE SCORE!

As you work through the activity, keep in mind that you will be earning a grade for the following.

- how well you work with the materials and equipment (30%)
- the quality and clarity of your observations (40%)
- how well you analyze the Coriolis effect in relationship to the Earth's axis and rotation (30%)

Using Scientific Methods

ASK QUESTIONS

In what directions does the Coriolis effect take place?

How does the Coriolis effect influence ocean currents?

MATERIALS AND EQUIPMENT

- one-quarter sheet of poster board
- full sheet of foam board larger than the poster board
- crayon or marker
- pushpin
- scissors
- a marble
- a partner to help you make and record your observations

SAFETY INFORMATION 

- Instruct students on basic safety with scissors and pointed objects such as pushpins.
- Do not eat or drink anything in the laboratory.

MAKE AND OBSERVE A MODEL

1. Write the letter N (for North) in the center of the poster board. In the center of the other side, write the letter S (for South). Hold the board and rotate it counterclockwise, with the N side facing up. Have your partner sit or kneel under the board and observe the S. In what direction is the S rotating, compared to the N?

   When seen from underneath, the board appears to be rotating in the oppo-

   site direction than when seen from above.

Name _____________________________ Class _____________ Date __________

Performance-Based Assessment *continued*

2. Make a hole large enough for your finger near one edge of the poster board. Use the tip of a closed pair of scissors to enlarge the hole. Push the pushpin through the center of the board and into the foam board.

3. Put your finger in the finger hole and slowly rotate the board counterclockwise. Have your partner roll the marble across the board, making sure the marble doesn't hit your finger. Describe the path the marble takes.

The marble curves to the right.

4. While still rotating the board counterclockwise, try rolling the marble in a few different directions. Describe what happens.

The marble curves to the right.

FORM A HYPOTHESIS

5. What will happen if you rotate the board counterclockwise?

The marble will curve in the direction opposite to the rotation; that is, to

the left.

TEST THE HYPOTHESIS

6. Rotate the board clockwise. Which pole does the center of the board now represent?

The center of the board now represents the South Pole.

7. While you rotate the board clockwise, have your partner roll the marble again, from different directions. Describe the path the marble takes.

As long as the direction of the rotation is clockwise, the marble curves to

the left.

DRAW CONCLUSIONS

8. Relate what you have observed in this activity to ocean currents.

Sample answer: Because the Earth is rotating on its axis, ocean water

behaves like the marble, traveling in curved paths. this is called the Coriolis

effect. In the Northern Hemisphere, the water curves to the right, and in the

Southern Hemisphere it curves to the left. Bonus answer: The Earth rotates

from west to east, so this force moves ocean currents at the equator from

east to west.

Skills Practice Lab

DATASHEET FOR CHAPTER LAB

Up from the Depths

Teacher Notes and Answer Key

TIME REQUIRED

One 45-minute class period.

Gordon Zibelman
Drexel Hill Middle School
Drexel Hill, Pennsylvania

LAB RATINGS

Easy ◄——1——2——3——4——► Hard

Teacher Prep–1
Student Set-Up–3
Concept Level–2
Clean Up–1

MATERIALS

The materials listed on the student page are enough for a group of 4-5 students. Note that the food coloring is used only to distinguish the water layers. Any two colors will work. You may find it simpler to make a roll of plastic wrap available to the class. Groups can then take a piece when they reach the appropriate steps.

SAFETY CAUTION

Remind students to review all safety cautions and icons before beginning this lab activity.

Name _______________________________ Class _______________ Date _____________

DATASHEET FOR CHAPTER LAB

Up from the Depths

Every year, the water in certain parts of the ocean "turns over." That is, the water at the bottom rises to the top and the water at the top falls to the bottom. This yearly change brings fresh nutrients from the bottom of the ocean to the fish living near the surface. However, the water in some parts of the ocean never turns over. By completing this activity, you will find out why not.

Keep in mind that some parts of the ocean are warmer at the bottom, and some are warmer at the top. And sometimes the saltiest water is at the bottom and sometimes not. As you complete this activity, you will investigate how these factors help determine whether the water will turn over.

OBJECTIVES

Demonstrate the effects of temperature and salinity on the density of water.

Describe why some parts of the ocean turn over, while others do not.

MATERIALS

- beakers, 400 mL (5)
- blue and red food coloring
- bucket of ice
- gloves, heat-resistant
- plastic wrap, 4 pieces, approximately 30.cm × 20 cm
- hot plate
- salt
- spoon
- tap water
- watch or clock

SAFETY INFORMATION

Using Scientific Methods

ASK A QUESTION

1. Why do some parts of the ocean turn over and not others?

____

____

FORM A HYPOTHESIS

2. Write a hypothesis that is a possible answer to the question above. Explain your reasoning.

____

____

____

Name _______________________________ Class _______________ Date ____________

Up from the Depths *continued*

TEST THE HYPOTHESIS

3. Label the beakers 1 through 5. Fill beakers 1 through 4 with tap water.

4. Add a drop of blue food coloring to the water in beakers 1 and 2, and stir with the spoon.

5. Place beaker 1 in the bucket of ice for 10 min.

6. Add a drop of red food coloring to the water in beakers 3 and 4, and stir with the spoon.

7. Set beaker 3 on a hot plate turned to a low setting for 10 min.

8. Add one spoonful of salt to the water in beaker 4, and stir with the spoon.

9. While beaker 1 is cooling and beaker 3 is heating, copy the observations table below on a sheet of paper.

Observations Table	
Mixture of water	**Observations**
Warm water placed above cold water	
Cold water placed above warm water	
Salty water placed above fresh water	
Fresh water placed above salty water	

10. Pour half of the water in beaker 1 into beaker 5. Return beaker 1 to the bucket of ice.

11. Tuck a sheet of plastic wrap into beaker 5 so that the plastic rests on the surface of the water and lines the upper half of the beaker.

12. Put on your gloves. Slowly pour half of the water in beaker 3 into the plastic-lined upper half of beaker 5 to form two layers of water. Return beaker 3 to the hot plate, and remove your gloves.

13. Very carefully, pull on one edge of the plastic wrap and remove it so that the warm, red water rests on the cold, blue water.

Caution: The plastic wrap may be warm.

14. Wait about 5 minutes, and then observe the layers in beaker 5. Did one layer remain on top of the other? Was there any mixing or turning over? Record your observations in your observations table.

The warm, red water remained on top of the cold, blue water. There was very

little mixing (if any), and there was no turning over.

15. Empty beaker 5, and rinse it with clean tap water.

Name _______________________________ Class ______________ Date ______________

▌Up from the Depths *continued*

16. Repeat the procedure used in steps 10–15. This time, pour warm, red water from beaker 3 on the bottom and cold, blue water from beaker 1 on top. (Use gloves when pouring warm water.)

The cold, blue water did not remain on top of the warm, red water. There was very little mixing (if any), and the water turned over.

17. Again, repeat the procedure used in steps 10–15. This time, pour blue tap water from beaker 2 on the bottom and red, salty water from beaker 4 on top.

The red, salty water did not remain on top of the blue tap water. There was little mixing, and the water turned over.

18. Repeat the procedure used in steps 10–15 a third time. This time, pour red, salty water from beaker 4 on the bottom and blue tap water from beaker 2 on top.

The blue tap water remained on top of the red, salty water. There was little mixing, and the water did not turn over.

ANALYZE THE RESULTS

1. Analyzing Data Compare the results of all four trials. Explain why the water turned over in some of the trials but not in all of them.

In each case, the denser water sank to the bottom. Cold water is denser than warm water. When put in a beaker with warm water, the cold water either stayed at the bottom or sank to the bottom. Salt water is denser than fresh water. When put in a beaker with fresh water, the saltwater either stayed at the bottom or sank to the bottom.

DRAW CONCLUSIONS

2. Evaluating Results What is the effect of temperature and salinity on the density of water?

The density of water increases as its temperature decreases—cold water is denser than warm water. The density of water increases as its salinity increases—salt water is denser than fresh water.

Name _______________________________ Class _______________ Date _______________

Up from the Depths *continued*

3. **Drawing Conclusions** What makes the temperature of ocean water decrease? What could make the salinity of ocean water increase?

The temperature of water can decrease because of seasonal temperature

fluctuations or cold wind blowing across the water's surface. Currents can

also carry cooler water to an area. The salinity of water can increase when

evaporation occurs or when ice forms on the water's surface. These

processes leave salts behind and make the remaining water denser.

4. **Drawing Conclusions** What reasons can you give to explain why some parts of the ocean do not turn over in the spring while some do?

Parts of the ocean that turn over do so because their density changes due to

variations in salinity or temperature. Parts of the ocean that do not turn

over must not experience significant variations in salinity or temperature.

APPLYING YOUR DATA

Suggest a method for setting up a model that tests the combined effects of temperature and salinity on the density of water. Consider using more than two water samples and dyes.

The following combinations could be used:

Top	Bottom
salt/cold	**fresh/warm**
salt/warm	**fresh/cold**
fresh/cold	**salt/warm**
fresh/warm	**salt/cold**

Name _______________________________ Class _______________ Date _______________

                                    DATASHEET FOR QUICK LAB

Doing the Wave

1. Tie one end of a **thin piece of rope** to a **doorknob**.

2. Tie a **ribbon** around the rope halfway between the doorknob and the other end of the rope.

3. Holding the rope at the untied end, quickly move the rope up and down and observe the ribbon.

4. How does the movement of the rope and ribbon relate to the movement of water and deep-water waves?

   Sample answer: As wave energy passed through the rope, the ribbon moved

   up and down, but it did not move closer to the doorknob. Similarly, wave

   energy passes through water, moving it up and down, but it does not trans-

   port water.

5. Repeat step 3, but move the rope higher and lower this time.

6. How does this affect the waves in the rope?

   Sample answer: The wave height increased, but wavelength decreased—more

   waves occurred along the same length of rope.

DATASHEET FOR LABBOOK

Turning the Tides

Teacher Notes and Answer Key

TIME REQUIRED

One 45-minute class period

Tracy Jahn
Berkshire Jr.-Sr. High
Canaan, New York

LAB RATINGS

Teacher Prep–2
Student Set-Up–3
Concept Level–3
Clean Up–1

MATERIALS

The materials listed on the student page are enough for a group of 2 to 4 students.

SAFETY INFORMATION

Safety Caution Remind students to review all safety cautions and icons before beginning this lab activity. Students should wear safety goggles. Be sure that students have enough space to spin the system.

PREPARATION NOTES

You will need to put a mark at the center of all of the cardboard disks. Students will need to draw the radius of the circle from the center to the edge of the disk. Encourage students to draw this line along the corrugations of the cardboard. Otherwise, several other steps will be made more difficult. The cardboard disks are not to scale with the Earth and moon. They are used to show how a two-body system, such as the Earth-moon system, rotates. The disks must be different sizes. The large disks could be 10 cm in diameter, and the smaller disks could be 5 cm in diameter.

Name _______________________________ Class _________________ Date _____________

DATASHEET FOR LABBOOK

Turning the Tides

Daily tides are caused by two "bulges" on the ocean's surface—one on the side of the Earth facing the moon and the other on the opposite side of the Earth. The bulge on the side facing the moon is caused by the moon's gravitational pull on the water. But the bulge on the opposite side of the Earth is slightly more difficult to explain. Whereas the moon pulls the water on one side of the Earth, the combined rotation of the Earth and the moon "pushes" the water on the opposite side of the Earth. In this activity, you will model the motion of the Earth and the moon to investigate the tidal bulge on the side of Earth facing away from the moon.

MATERIALS

- cardboard, 1 cm × 1 cm piece
- corrugated cardboard, one large and one small, with centers marked (2 disks)
- dowel, 1/4 in. in diameter and 36 cm long
- glue, white
- pencil, sharp
- stapler with staples
- string, 5 cm length

SAFETY INFORMATION 

PROCEDURE

1. Draw a line from the center of each disk along the folds in the cardboard to the edge of the disk. This line is the radius.

2. Place a drop of white glue on one end of the dowel. Lay the larger disk flat, and align the dowel with the line for the radius you drew in step 1. Insert about 2.5 cm of the dowel into the edge of the disk.

3. Add a drop of glue to the other end of the dowel, and push that end into the smaller disk, again along its radius. The setup should look like a large, two-headed lollipop. This setup is a model of the Earth-moon system.

4. Staple the string to the edge of the large disk on the side opposite the dowel. Staple the cardboard square to the other end of the string. This smaller piece of cardboard represents the Earth's oceans that face away from the moon.

5. Place the tip of the pencil at the center of the large disk and spin the model. You may poke a small hole in the bottom of the disk with your pencil, but DO NOT poke all the way through the cardboard. Record your observations.
Caution: Be sure you are at a safe distance from other people before spinning your model.

Name _______________________________ Class _______________ Date _______________

Turning the Tides *continued*

6. Now, find your model's center of mass. The center of mass is the point at which the model can be balanced on the end of the pencil. (Hint: It might be easier to find the center of mass by using the eraser end. Then, use the sharpened end of the pencil to balance the model.) This balance point should be just inside the edge of the larger disk.

7. Place the pencil at the center of mass, and spin the model around the pencil. Again, you may wish to poke a small hole in the disk. Record your observations.

ANALYZE THE RESULTS

1. What happened when you tried to spin the model around the center of the large disk? This model, called the Earth-centered model, represents the incorrect view that the moon orbits the center of the Earth.

Answers may vary. Sample answer: When I tried to spin the model around the center of the large disk, I could not get the model to balance on the pencil.

2. What happened when you tried to spin the model around its center of mass? This point, called the barycenter, is the point around which both the Earth and the moon rotate.

Answers may vary. Sample answer: I was able to balance the model at the barycenter. The model spun, and the small piece of cardboard on the string swung outward.

3. In each case, what happened to the string and cardboard square when the model was spun?

Answers may vary. Sample answer: The cardboard square hung down when I tried to swing the model around the center of the large disk; I was unable to make the model spin. When I spun the model around its barycenter, the square swung away from the model.

Name _______________________________ Class _______________ Date _______________

Turning the Tides *continued*

DRAW CONCLUSIONS

4. Which model—the Earth-centered model or the barycentric model—explains why the Earth has a tidal bulge on the side opposite the moon? Explain your answer.

The barycentric model explains why the Earth has a bulge on the side oppo-

site the moon. The side of the Earth opposite the side facing the moon acts

in much the same way the small square of cardboard does in this model. As

the Earth-moon system rotates, the side of the Earth facing away from the

moon bulges outward.

Answer Key

Directed Reading A

SECTION: CURRENTS

1. ocean currents
2. rotation, continents
3. from Peru to an island in Polynesia
4. Heyerdahl was trying to prove that ocean currents had carried the ancient Peruvians across the Pacific Ocean to Polynesia.
5. surface currents
6. Near the poles, surface currents move from west to east. Near the equator, they move east to west.
7. Wind and surface currents appear to move in curved paths because of the rotation of the Earth.
8. the Coriolis effect
9. The surface current deflects, or changes direction.
10. Cold-water currents begin near the poles. Warm-water currents begin near the equator.
11. B
12. C
13. D
14. A
15. E
16. because it is colder
17. As the ice freezes, dissolved solids are squeezed out into the water below. This increases the salinity, and therefore the density, of the water.
18. Evaporation removes water molecules but leaves solids behind. This increases both the salinity and the density of the water.
19. A deep current is colder.
20. A deep current has a higher saline content.

SECTION: CURRENTS AND CLIMATE

1. B
2. A
3. C
4. D
5. B
6. C
7. D
8. El Niño and La Niña form in the Pacific Ocean.
9. During El Niño, the surface temperature of the Pacific Ocean gets warmer.
10. During La Niña, the surface temperature of the Pacific Ocean gets colder.
11. Answers will vary. Sample answer: The changes in weather caused by El Niño can result in heavy rains in places that are usually dry. The rains can cause flash floods and mudslides. El Niño also can cause drought in places where there is usually rain. Crops can fail during these droughts.
12. because of its effects on organisms and land
13. data about surface temperature, air temperature, currents, and winds

SECTION: WAVES

1. crest, trough
2. wavelength
3. wave height
4. the wind
5. As waves of energy pass through the water, the water rises and falls in circular movements. The wave of energy passes through the water. The water itself stays behind.
6. wave period
7. wave speed
8. B
9. D
10. A
11. K
12. F
13. I
14. C
15. J
16. G
17. H
18. E

SECTION: TIDES

1. Tides are periodic changes in the water level of oceans and other large bodies of water.
2. sun and moon
3. A
4. B
5. C

6. B

7. D

8. tidal range

9. spring

10. neap

11. a body of water that rushes up through a narrow bay, estuary, or river channel during the rise of high tide and causes a very sudden tidal rise

12. in coastal areas of China, the British Isles, France, and Canada

13. the Bay of Fundy, in New Brunswick, Canada

Directed Reading B

SECTION: CURRENTS

1. water

2. weather

3. continents

4. D

5. A

6. B

7. A

8. D

9. B

10. A

11. B

12. C

13. C

14. C

15. B

SECTION: CURRENTS AND CLIMATE

1. B

2. A

3. B

4. C

5. D

6. A

7. B

8. C

SECTION: WAVES

1. A

2. B

3. D

4. C

5. A

6. D

7. B

8. C

9. B

10. B

11. C

12. A

13. D

14. C

15. A

16. D

17. C

18. A

19. C

SECTION: TIDES

1. A

2. C

3. A

4. C

5. D

6. B

7. A

8. D

Vocabulary and Section Summary

CURRENTS

1. An ocean current is a movement of ocean water that follows a regular pattern.

2. A surface current is a horizontal movement of ocean water that is caused by wind and that occurs on or near the ocean's surface.

3. The Coriolis effect is the apparent curving of the path of a moving object from an otherwise straight path due to the Earth's rotation.

4. A deep current is a streamlike movement of ocean water far below the surface.

CURRENTS AND CLIMATE

1. Upwelling is the movement of deep, cold, and nutrient-rich water to the surface.

2. El Niño is a change in the water temperature in the Pacific Ocean that produces a warm current.

3. La Niña is a change in the eastern Pacific Ocean in which the surface water temperatures become unusually cool.

WAVES

1. An undertow is a subsurface current that is near shore and that pulls objects out to sea.

2. A longshore current is a water current that travels near and parallel to the shoreline.

3. A whitecap is the bubbles in the crest of a breaking wave.

4. A swell is one of a group of long ocean waves that have steadily traveled a great distance from their point of origin.

5. A tsunami is a giant ocean wave that forms after a volcanic eruption, submarine earthquake, or landslide.

6. A storm surge is a local rise in sea level near the shore that is caused by strong winds from a storm, such as those from a hurricane.

TIDES

1. A tide is the periodic rise and fall of the water level in the oceans and other large bodies of water.

2. The tidal range is the difference in levels of ocean water at high tide and low tide.

3. A spring tide is a tide of increased range that occurs two times a month, at the new and full moons.

4. A neap tide is a tide of minimum range that occurs during the first and third quarters of the moon.

Section Review

CURRENTS

1. Surface currents

2. deep currents

3. D

4. Global winds, the Coriolis effect, continental deflections

5. When a surface current meets a continent, the surface current will *deflect*, or change direction.

6. Decreasing the water's temperature or increasing its salinity will increase its density. As water becomes more dense, it sinks and becomes a deep current that moves along the ocean floor.

7. $90{,}000{,}000$ mi^3/s $-$ $40{,}000.000$ mi^3/s $=$ $50{,}000{,}000$ mi^3/s

8. Sample answer: If there were no land on Earth's surface, surface currents would not deflect sharply, as they do when they contact continents.

9. Sample answer: Surface currents are streamlike movements of water at or near the surface of the ocean. Deep currents are streamlike movements of ocean water located far below the surface. Global winds, the Coriolis effect, and continental deflections contribute to the formation of surface currents. Deep currents form where the density of ocean water increases.

CURRENTS AND CLIMATE

1. Sample answer: Upwelling is a process in which cold, nutrient-rich water from the deep ocean rises to the surface. An El Niño can alter weather patterns enough to cause disasters. A La Niña can cause surface water temperatures to become unusually cool.

2. C

3. Even though Scotland is located at a high latitude, its climate is relatively mild because the Gulf Stream carries warm water from the Tropics to the North Atlantic Ocean.

4. El Niño can cause flash floods and landslides.

5. 81 kg

6. Sample answer: During El Niño, upwelling does not occur along the coast of Peru. When upwelling does not occur, nutrients from deep water do not rise to the surface. Marine organisms that depend on the nutrients for food may die or move to other areas in search of food. Fishers who depend on these organisms may have reduced catch, which will negatively affect fishers' way of life.

WAVES

1. Sample answer: A whitecap is a wave that is white and foamy and has very steep crests that break in the open ocean. Swells are rolling waves that move steadily across the ocean.

2. Sample answer: An undertow is a movement of water, which carries sand, rock particles, and plankton away from the shoreline. A longshore current is a water current that travels near and parallel to the shoreline.

3. Sample answer: A tsunami is a giant ocean wave that forms after a volcanic eruption, submarine earthquake, or landslide. A storm surge is a local rise in sea level near the shore that is caused by a storm, such as a hurricane.

4. B

5. Deep-water waves become shallow-water waves as they move toward the shore.

6. Water at or near the surface rises and falls in circular movements as waves move through it.

7. underwater earthquakes, volcanic eruptions, landslides, underwater explosions, or the impact of a meteorite or comet

8. The crest is the highest point of a wave, and the trough is the lowest point of a wave.

9. about 167 years

10. A floating bottle remains in the same spot as waves travel from left to right. If the bottle moves in the same direction as the waves, it is moving because of a surface current. Student drawings should look similar to Figure 2 but should include a surface current.

11. As a wave approaches the shore, wave height increases and causes the wave to crash into the ocean floor. Then, wave height decreases and the wave continues to break until it reaches the shore.

12. Waves are created when energy is transferred to the water as wind blows across the water's surface.

13. An undertow forms when waves crash on the beach head-on. A longshore current forms when waves hit the shore at an angle. An undertow carries sand away from the shoreline while a longshore current carries sand down the shoreline.

TIDES

1. Sample answer: Spring tides have maximum tidal range and occur every 14 days. Neap tides have minimum tidal range and occur during the first and third quarters of the moon.

2. A

3. Neap tides have minimum tidal range, and spring tides have maximum tidal range.

4. The combined forces of the sun and the moon on the Earth result in tidal ranges that vary based on the positions of all three bodies.

5. 1,490 minutes

6. Seven days pass between the maximum and minimum tidal ranges in any given area. Both spring tides and neap tides occur every 14 days. Neap tides occur halfway between the occurrence of spring tides, and vice versa. Therefore, midway between the cycle of each type of tide, the other type of tide occurs. The two types of tide as alternate every 7 days.

7. High tides occur on the side of Earth facing the moon and on the side of Earth opposite the moon. When high tides occur, low tides form on the sides of Earth that are not facing or opposite the moon.

Chapter Review

1. Sample answer: Surface currents are streamlike movements of water that occur on or near the surface of the ocean. Deep currents are streamlike movements of ocean water far below the surface.

2. Sample answer: An El Niño is a change in the water temperature of the Pacific Ocean that produces a warm current. A La Niña is a change in the eastern Pacific Ocean in which the surface water temperature becomes unusually cool.

3. Sample answer: A spring tide is a tide of increased range that occurs during the full and new moons. A neap tide is a tide of minimum tidal range that occurs during the first and third quarters of the moon.

4. Sample answer: A tide is the periodic rise and fall of the water level in oceans and other large bodies of water. Tidal range is the difference in levels of ocean water at high and low tide.

5. D

6. D

7. C

8. A

9. C

10. A

11. When El Niño occurs, warm surface water remains along the Pacific Coast of South America. Therefore, upwelling does not occur along the coast.

12. A crest is the highest point of a wave and a trough is the lowest point of a wave. The wavelength of a wave is the distance between two adjacent wave crests or troughs. Wave period is the time between the passage of two wave crests or troughs. Wavelength divided by wave period gives wave speed.

13. During neap tide, the sun, the moon, and the Earth form a right angle, with the Earth in the middle. During spring tide, the sun, moon, and Earth align in a straight line.

14. The breaker zone is where waves first begin to tumble downward. The surf is the zone between the breaker zone and the shore. In the surf, water moves toward the shore.

15. The Gulf Stream, which is a warm-water current, creates a relatively mild climate for the British Isles.

16. Deep currents form where the density of ocean water increases. Water density depends on temperature and salinity.

17. An answer to this exercise can be found at the end of this book.

18. Because the oceans are liquid, they flow more easily than land.

19. It is important to study El Niño and La Niña because both affect climate, land, and organisms.

20. 12:50 P.M. (The answer 1:15 A.M. is also acceptable.)

21. Global winds blow across the Earth's surface, which creates surface currents in the ocean. The Coriolis effect is the apparent curving of moving objects from a straight path due to the Earth's rotation. Therefore the rotation of the Earth causes ocean currents to curve as they move across the Earth's surface. Continental deflections occur when a surface current comes into contact with a continent. This causes the surface current to deflect, or change direction.

22. Answers may vary. Sample answer: Any two currents listed by red arrows are acceptable as warm-water currents. Any two currents listed as blue arrows are acceptable as cold-water currents.

23. Sample answer: The Labrador Current would most likely bring a cool climate to Canada and Greenland because it's a cold-water current.

Reinforcement

GOING WITH THE FLOW

1. Answers will vary. Sample answer: San Francisco, California

2. Answers will vary. Sample answer: the California Current

3. Answers will vary. Sample answer: California Current, North Equatorial Current, west along equator through islands to Indian Ocean, west across Indian Ocean to East Africa, south along coast, around tip of Africa, north on Benguela Current, west on South Equatorial Current, south along coast, around tip of South America, north on Peru current, north along California coast

4. Answers will vary. Sample answer: The Equatorial Countercurrent flows just south of the North Equatorial Current. There are countercurrents in the Indian Ocean and along the southeastern coast of South America. The Peru Current meets the Equatorial Countercurrent off the west coast of South America.

5. Answers will vary. Sample answer: The North Equatorial Current is deflected by a chain of islands in the southeastern Pacific. The South Equatorial Current is deflected by South America.

6. Answers will vary. Sample answer: Currents form large circles in the South Indian, South Atlantic, and South Pacific Oceans.

7. Currents coming from the pole cool the water off southern Africa and southern South America (the Benguala and Peru Currents).

8. Answers will vary. Sample answer: I sailed west across the Pacific Ocean on the North Equatorial Current. When I reached the islands, I turned south toward Australia, then followed a westward current across the Indian Ocean. I turned south along the coast of Africa, then caught the Benguala and South Equatorial Currents across the South Atlantic Ocean. I battled my way down the coast and around South America, then caught the Peru Current North. I sailed close to the shore of North America and reached home.

Reinforcement

MASTERING THE WAVES

1. Answers will vary. Sample answer: Date varies, swells, whitecaps

2. Answers will vary. Sample answer: Date varies, trough, crest

3. Answers will vary. Sample answer: Date varies, wave height

4. Answers will vary. Sample answer: Date varies, breakers, surf, undertow

5. Answers will vary. Sample answer: Date varies, tsunamis

6. Answers will vary. Sample answer: Date varies, storm surges

Critical Thinking

1. As waves approach the shore, they increase in height. This happens because of interaction between the water and the ocean floor. As deep-water waves become shallow-water waves, the water particles slow down and build up. This change forces more water between wave crests, which increases wave height.

2. After a wave crashes into the surf, the water flows back to the ocean underneath incoming waves, creating an undertow.

3. The cruise ship is in no danger because the wave height in the open ocean is only 2m. As the waves approach the coast their amplitude will increase, creating huge, devastating breakers.

4. When the waves move ashore, they could flood homes, wash boats ashore, uproot trees, and erode the coastline.

5. After the waves of the tsunami hit the shore, they will create a giant undertow that will cause even more damage and danger.

6. The waves of the tsunami will not push the ship ashore because the water in waves moves in vertical circles. Wave energy moves through the water, creating the troughs and crests of the waves. The wave simply raises and lowers the ship.

7. When there is a tsunami warning, people in coastal areas should move inland.

8. When there is a tsunami warning, ships at sea should move into deeper water.

Section Quizzes

SECTION: CURRENTS

1. A	**6.** D
2. C	**7.** B
3. C	**8.** C
4. A	**9.** B
5. B	**10.** C

SECTION: CURRENTS AND CLIMATE

1. B	**6.** I
2. J	**7.** D
3. H	**8.** F
4. E	**9.** C
5. A	**10.** G

SECTION: WAVES

1. C	**6.** C
2. B	**7.** B
3. B	**8.** D
4. B	**9.** A
5. C	**10.** C

SECTION: TIDES

1. J	**6.** G
2. A	**7.** I
3. D	**8.** F
4. B	**9.** E
5. C	**10.** H

Chapter Test A

1. C	**13.** A
2. B	**14.** F
3. A	**15.** E
4. C	**16.** B
5. C	**17.** D
6. D	**18.** C
7. B	**19.** A
8. A	**20.** C
9. C	**21.** B
10. B	**22.** D
11. C	**23.** B
12. D	**24.** C

Chapter Test B

1. surface currents
2. deep currents
3. El Niño
4. wavelength
5. tidal range
6. A
7. C
8. C
9. D
10. A
11. global winds, the Coriolis effect, continental deflections
12. density, salinity, and temperature; accept also the Coriolis effect.
13. buoys, satellites
14. As deep-water waves become shallow-water waves, the water particles slow down and build up. This change forces more water between wave crests, which increases wave height.
15. During spring tides, the gravity of the sun and pull on the Earth either from the same direction or from opposite directions, producing higher tidal ranges. During neap tides, the sun and moon are at right angles with respect to Earth. This lessens their pull on Earth, producing lower tidal ranges.
16. Winds and currents flow faster at the equator than at the poles. One reason equatorial currents are faster is that they are warmer. Another reason is that the speed of the Earth's rotation is much faster at the equator. (A point near the poles and a point at the equator both rotate in 24 hours, but the point at the equator has traveled a much greater distance in that time.)
17. If El Niño prevents an upwelling, nutrients from the ocean floor are not brought up to the surface. This deprives tiny shore plants and animals of nutrients and harms the shoreline ecosystem.
18. Breakers form as waves interact with the ocean floor. Undertows are moving out to sea along the ocean floor. Therefore undertows must contribute to the slowing down of incoming waves and the buildup of water molecules that cause the waves to increase in height.
19. People in coastal areas should learn about tides and waves in order to predict the best times for using the beach, to prevent accidents, and to stay alert for dangers, such as storm surges.
20. **a.** deep-water waves
    b. swells
    c. breakers
    d. surf
    e. undertow

Chapter Test C

1. B
2. A
3. B
4. A
5. C
6. B
7. D
8. A
9. B
10. D
11. C
12. A
13. B
14. C
15. D
16. C

17. B
18. D
19. A
20. wave period
21. breakers
22. tsunamis
23. moon
24. tides
25. tidal bore

Standardized Test Preparation

READING

Passage 1
1. B
2. I

Passage 2
1. D
2. G

INTERPRETING GRAPHICS
1. B
2. F
3. C

MATH
1. D
2. F
3. A
4. F

Vocabulary Activity

O	C	E	A	N	S	C	U	R	R	E	N	T	S	S
N	O	A	A	W	A	V	E	L	E	N	G	T	H	U
P	R	S	W	W	L	O	N	G	S	H	O	R	E	N
A	I	T	A	H	I	N	D	E	N	S	I	T	Y	S
C	O	N	T	I	N	E	N	T	A	L	D	E	E	P
I	L	B	E	T	T	A	U	P	O	L	E	S	C	R
F	I	R	R	E	Y	P	P	S	U	R	F	U	R	I
I	S	E	D	C	P	T	W	W	N	T	L	R	E	N
C	E	A	R	A	E	I	E	T	D	S	E	F	S	G
S	F	K	O	P	R	D	L	R	E	U	C	A	T	E
W	F	E	U	S	I	E	L	O	R	N	T	C	R	L
E	E	R	G	T	O	J	I	U	T	A	I	E	A	N
L	C	S	H	O	D	J	N	G	O	M	O	O	N	I
L	T	C	T	R	H	I	G	H	W	I	N	D	G	Ñ
S	L	O	W	M	S	U	R	G	E	B	O	R	E	O

SciLinks Activity

1. North Pacific, Kuroshio, North Equatorial, South Equatorial Peru, Gulf Stream, West Wind Drift, East Wind Drift
2. The two largest ocean currents are the Antarctic Circumpolar Current, which circles Antarctica, and the Kuroshio Current, off the coast of Japan.
3. Ocean habitats include beaches, coral reefs, estuaries, hydrothermal vents, kelp forests, and sea grass beds.
4. The more pressure, the greater the density. Since pressure increases as you move down through the ocean, the density also increases the farther down you go.
5. Winds and currents are created by energy from the sun, which heats ocean waters more at the equator than at the poles. This creates convection currents.
6. In general, the temperatures of coastal areas are warmer and more moderate than the temperatures of nearby inland areas.

Lesson Plan

Section: Currents

Pacing

Regular Schedule: **with lab(s):** 2 days **without lab(s):** 1 day

Block Schedule: **with lab(s):** 1 day **without lab(s):** 0.5 day

Objectives

1. Describe surface currents.

2. List the three factors that control surface currents.

3. Describe deep currents.

4. Identify the three factors that form deep currents.

National Science Education Standards Covered

UCP 2: Evidence, models, and explanation

SAI 1: Abilities necessary to do scientific inquiry

HNS 1: Science as a human endeavor

HNS 3: History of science

ES 1j: Global patterns of atmospheric movement influence local weather. Oceans have a major effect on climate, because the water in the oceans holds a large amount of heat.

KEY

SE = Student Edition **TE** = Teacher's Edition
CRF = Chapter Resource File

FOCUS (*5 minutes*)

_ **Chapter Starter Transparency** Use this transparency to introduce the chapter.

_ **Bellringer, TE** Have students retrace the voyage of the *Kon-Tiki*, discuss Heyerdahl's theory, and explain the difference between a successful model and accurate proof.

_ **Bellringer Transparency** Use this transparency as students enter the classroom and find their seats.

MOTIVATE *(10 minutes)*

_ **Discussion, Rivers and Surface Currents, TE** Have students compare rivers and surface currents. (**GENERAL**)

_ **Connection Activity, Life Science, Current Colonies, TE** Have students create a poster that highlights the unique plants and animals of the Galápagos Islands. (**ADVANCED**)

TEACH *(65 minutes)*

_ **Reading Strategy, SE** Have students create outlines of the section as they read and summarize the text, using the heads and subheads as outline points. (**GENERAL**)

_ **Inclusion Strategies, TE** Demonstrate to students how surface currents move.

_ **Activity, The Coriolis Effect, TE** Use a turntable to demonstrate the Coriolis effect. (**BASIC/SPECIAL NEEDS**)

_ **Teaching Transparency, Earth's Rotation and Coriolis Effect** Use the graphic to illustrate Earth's rotation and the Coriolis effect.

_ **Directed Reading A/B, CRF** These worksheets reinforce basic concepts and vocabulary presented in the lesson. (**BASIC/SPECIAL NEEDS**)

_ **Vocabulary and Section Summary, CRF** Students write definitions of key terms and read a summary of section content. (**GENERAL**)

_ **Reinforcement, CRF** This worksheet reinforces key in the chapter. (**GENERAL**)

_ **Chapter Lab, CRF** Students try to discover why some parts of the ocean turn over, while others do not. (**GENERAL**)

_ **SciLinks Activity, Ocean Currents, Code HSM1061, CRF** Students research Internet sources related to ocean currents. (**GENERAL**)

CLOSE *(10 minutes)*

_ **Quiz, TE** Students answer 1 question about ocean currents. (**GENERAL**)

_ **Alternative Assessment, Sailing with the Currents, TE** Students plan a trip around the world that has them sail with the currents. (**GENERAL**)

_ **Reteaching, Movement of Ocean Currents TE** Ask students to list the three factors that control surface currents and the factors that cause deep currents to form. (**BASIC**)

_ **Section Review, SE** Students answer end-of-section vocabulary, key ideas, math, and critical thinking questions. (**GENERAL**)

_ **Section Quiz, CRF** Students answer 10 objective questions about ocean currents. (**GENERAL**)

Lesson Plan

Section: Currents and Climate

Pacing

Regular Schedule: **with lab(s):** N/A   **without lab(s):** 1 day

Block Schedule: **with lab(s):** N/A   **without lab(s):** 0.5 day

Objectives

1. Explain how currents affect climate.

2. Describe the effects of El Niño.

3. Explain how scientists study and predict the pattern of El Niño.

National Science Education Standards Covered

UCP 2: Evidence, models, and explanation

SAI 1: Abilities necessary to do scientific inquiry

ES 1j: Global patterns of atmospheric movement influence local weather. Oceans have a major effect on climate, because the water in the oceans holds a large amount of heat.

KEY
SE = Student Edition   **TE** = Teacher's Edition
CRF = Chapter Resource File

FOCUS *(5 minutes)*

_ **Bellringer, TE** Have students compare the average yearly temperatures for the Scilly Isles in England and Newfoundland, Canada, and explain the reason for the difference.

_ **Bellringer Transparency** Use this transparency as students enter the classroom and find their seats.

MOTIVATE *(10 minutes)*

_ **Discussion, The Effects of Currents, TE** Ask students to brainstorm and discuss ways in which currents can affect climate. **(GENERAL)**

_ **Activity, Graphing Temperatures, TE** Have students graph average temperatures of coastal and inland cities and generalize about how ocean temperatures affect the climate of coastal areas. **(GENERAL)**

TEACH *(20 minutes)*

_ **Reading Strategy, SE** Have pairs of students read the section silently and take turns summarizing the material and discussing difficult concepts. **(GENERAL)**

_ **Reteaching, TE** Students list the various effects that currents can have on climate, land, and organisms. **(BASIC)**

_ **Brainfood, Surface Currents and Hurricanes, TE** Have students use the California Current to explain why no hurricane has ever made landfall in California. **(GENERAL)**

_ **Connection Activity, Real World, El Niño, TE** Students search for news stories describing some of the effects of El Niño in recent years. **(GENERAL)**

_ **Directed Reading A/B, CRF** These worksheets reinforce basic concepts and vocabulary presented in the lesson. **(BASIC/SPECIAL NEEDS)**

_ **Vocabulary and Section Summary, CRF** Have students write definitions of key terms and read a summary of section content. **(GENERAL)**

_ **Teaching Transparency, Upwelling** Use this graphic to illustrate upwelling.

CLOSE *(10 minutes)*

_ **Quiz, TE** Students answer 4 questions about currents and climate. **(GENERAL)**

_ **Alternative Assessment, Studying El Niño, TE** Ask students to write reports about how data that scientists collect about El Niño can help prevent future disasters. **(GENERAL)**

_ **Section Review, CRF** Students answer end-of-section vocabulary, key ideas, math, and critical thinking questions. **(GENERAL)**

_ **Section Quiz, CRF** Students answer 10 objective questions about currents and climate. **(GENERAL)**

Lesson Plan

Section: Waves

Pacing

Regular Schedule: **with lab(s):** N/A   **without lab(s):** 1 day

Block Schedule: **with lab(s):** N/A   **without lab(s):** 0.5 day

Objectives

1. Identify the parts of a wave.

2. Explain how the parts of a wave relate to wave movement.

3. Describe how ocean waves form and move.

4. Classify types of waves.

National Science Education Standards Covered

UCP 1: Systems, order, and organization

UCP 2: Evidence, models, and explanation

UCP 3: Change, constancy, and measurement

SAI 1: Abilities necessary to do scientific inquiry

SPSP 3: Natural hazards

SPSP 4: Risks and benefits

ES 1b: Lithospheric plates on the scales of continents and oceans constantly move at rates of centimeters per year in response to movements in the mantle. Major geological events, such as earthquakes, volcanic eruptions, and mountain building result from these plate motions.

KEY
SE = Student Edition   **TE** = Teacher's Edition
CRF = Chapter Resource File

FOCUS (*5 minutes*)

_ **Bellringer, TE** Ask students to hypothesize about whether floating objects would travel with currents or waves.

_ **Bellringer Transparency** Use this transparency as students enter the classroom and find their seats.

_ **Reading Strategy, SE** Have students write the titles of the headings in the section and predict what they will learn under each heading. (**GENERAL**)

MOTIVATE *(10 minutes)*

_ **Demonstration, Making Waves, TE** Have students suggest and demonstrate ways to move water in a tub without touching the water. (**GENERAL**)

_ **Group Activity, Modeling Waves, TE** Have students stand and make "human waves" by repeating the same motion in sequence. (**BASIC**)

TEACH *(20 minutes)*

_ **Connection Activity, Math, Wavelength and Wave Period, TE** Ask students to estimate and measure wavelength and wave periods. (**GENERAL**)

_ **Inclusion Strategies, TE** Have students create a wave bottle.

_ **Reading Strategy, Types of Waves, TE** Have students reproduce diagrams from the text in their science journals. (**BASIC/SPECIAL NEEDS**)

_ **Brainfood, Offshore Breakers, TE** Have students discuss why sighting offshore breakers might cause sailors to turn their boats around. (**GENERAL**)

_ **Connection Activity, Real World, Water Safety**, **TE** Instruct students on what to do if caught in an undertow. (**GENERAL**)

_ **Quick Lab, CRF** Students hold the untied end of a rope or ribbon and shake the rope up and down to observe wave movement. (**GENERAL**)

_ **Connection to Environmental Science, Beach Nourishment, TE** Have students investigate dredging, erosion, and other natural and human causes of changes to the shoreline. (**GENERAL**)

_ **Directed Reading A/B, CRF** These worksheets reinforce basic concepts and vocabulary presented in the lesson. (**BASIC/SPECIAL NEEDS**)

_ **Vocabulary and Section Summary, CRF** Have students write definitions of key terms and read a summary of section content. (**GENERAL**)

_ **Reinforcement, CRF** This worksheet reinforces key concepts in the chapter. (**GENERAL**)

_ **Critical Thinking, CRF** Ask students to fill out the worksheet about tsunamis. (**ADVANCED**)

CLOSE *(10 minutes)*

_ **Quiz, TE** Students create a concept map of section contents and vocabulary. (**GENERAL**)

_ **Alternative Assessment, TE** Students construct diagrams of various kinds of waves. (**GENERAL**)

_ **Section Review, CRF** Students answer end-of-section vocabulary, key ideas, math, and critical thinking questions. (**GENERAL**)

_ **Section Quiz, CRF** Students answer 10 objective questions about waves. (**GENERAL**)

Lesson Plan

Section: Tides

Pacing

Regular Schedule:	**with lab(s):** N/A	**without lab(s):** 1 day
Block Schedule:	**with lab(s):** N/A	**without lab(s):** 0.5 day

Objectives

1. Explain tides and their relationship with the Earth, sun, and moon.

2. Describe four different types of tides.

3. Analyze the relationship between tides and coastal land.

National Science Education Standards Covered

SAI 1: Abilities necessary to do scientific inquiry

ST 1: Abilities of technological design

HNS 1: Science as a human endeavor

HNS 3: History of science

ES 3c: Gravity is the force that keeps planets in orbit around the sun and governs the rest of the motion in the solar system. Gravity alone holds us to the earth's surface and explains the phenomena of the tides.

KEY
SE = Student Edition   TE = Teacher's Edition
CRF = Chapter Resource File

FOCUS *(5 minutes)*

_ **Bellringer, TE** Ask students to hypothesize about why the moon, although much smaller than the sun, exerts a much greater gravitational pull on the Earth.

_ **Bellringer Transparency** Use this transparency as students enter the classroom and find their seats.

MOTIVATE *(10 minutes)*

_ **Activity, Interial Zones, TE** Have students visit a tidal zone or research intertidal organisms and their survival strategies. (**GENERAL**)

TEACH *(20 minutes)*

_ **Using the Figure, Earth's Rotation, TE** Have students examine Figure 3 in detail and compare the rotation of the Earth and the revolution of the moon in terms of time. **(GENERAL)**

_ **Reading Strategy, SE** Have students form small groups, write down questions while reading the section in silence, then discuss the questions with their groups. **(GENERAL)**

_ **Discussion, Tide Discussion, TE** Students understand that the location of tides caries constantly. **(BASIC)**

_ **Activity, The Cause of Tides, TE** Use a small ball, a large ball, and a globe to demonstrate the revolution of the moon around the Earth and the rotation of the Earth. **(BASIC)**

_ **Directed Reading A/B, CRF** These worksheets reinforce basic concepts and vocabulary presented in the lesson. **(BASIC/SPECIAL NEEDS)**

_ **Vocabulary and Section Summary, CRF** Students write definitions of key terms and read a summary of section content. **(GENERAL)**

CLOSE *(10 minutes)*

_ **Quiz, TE** Students answer 1 question about tides. **(GENERAL)**

_ **Alternative Assessment, TE** Students draw tidal bulges based on random configurations of the Earth, moon, and sun. **(GENERAL)**

_ **Reteaching, Spring Tides and Neap Tides, TE** Have students reproduce Figure 4 in their science journals. **(GENERAL)**

_ **Section Review, CRF** Students answer end-of-section vocabulary, key ideas, math, and critical thinking questions. **(GENERAL)**

_ **Section Quiz, CRF** Students answer 10 objective questions about tides. **(GENERAL)**

Lesson Plan

End of Chapter Review and Assessment

Pacing

Regular Schedule: **with lab(s):** N/A   **without lab(s):** 2 days

Block Schedule: **with lab(s):** N/A   **without lab(s):** 1 day

---

KEY
SE = Student Edition   **TE** = Teacher's Edition
CRF = Chapter Resource File

_ **Chapter Review, CRF** Students answer end-of-chapter vocabulary, key ideas, critical thinking, and graphics questions. (**GENERAL**)

_ **Vocabulary Activity, CRF** Students review chapter vocabulary terms by finding 40 words in a hidden word puzzle. (**GENERAL**)

_ **Chapter Test A/B/C, CRF** Assign questions from the appropriate test for chapter assessment. (**GENERAL/ADVANCED/SPECIAL NEEDS**)

q **Performance-Based Asssessment, CRF** Assign this activity for general level assessment for the chapter. (**GENERAL**)

q **Standard Test Preparation, SE** Students answer reading comprehension, math, and interpreting graphics questions in the format of a standardized test. (**GENERAL**)

q **Test Generator, One-Stop Planner** Create a customized homework assignment, quiz, or test using the HRW Test Generator. (**GENERAL**)

_ **CNN Video, CNN Presents Science in the News: Scientists in Action,** Segment 20, "Mapping El Niño Erosion"

The Movement of Ocean Water

MULTIPLE CHOICE

1. Two examples of surface currents are the Gulf Stream and the
   a. Brazil Current.
   b. Antarctic Bottom Water.
   c. Coriolis effect.
   d. North Atlantic Deep Water.

   Answer: A Difficulty: 1 Section: 1 Objective: 3

2. Surface currents are caused by
   a. floods.
   b. warm water.
   c. the wind.
   d. the equator.

   Answer: C Difficulty: 1 Section: 1 Objective: 2

3. Ocean currents flow from east to west near the
   a. Gulf Stream.
   b. poles.
   c. equator.
   d. global winds.

   Answer: C Difficulty: 1 Section: 1 Objective: 2

4. The curved paths of global winds and surface currents are caused by
   a. the rotation of the Earth.
   b. the Coriolis effect.
   c. warm air near the equator.
   d. continental deflection.

   Answer: A Difficulty: 1 Section: 1 Objective: 2

5. Ocean currents in the Northern and Southern Hemispheres turn
   a. from west to east.
   b. in opposite directions.
   c. clockwise.
   d. against the Earth's rotation.

   Answer: B Difficulty: 1 Section: 1 Objective: 2

6. What does a surface current do when it deflects?
   a. gains speed
   b. moves toward cold water
   c. meets another ocean current
   d. changes direction

   Answer: D Difficulty: 1 Section: 1 Objective: 2

7. The density of ocean water increases when it
   a. joins the Gulf Stream.
   b. gets colder.
   c. gets warmer.
   d. turns to ice.

   Answer: B Difficulty: 1 Section: 1 Objective: 3

8. Which process increases the salinity of ocean water?
   a. the Coriolis effect
   b. convection currents
   c. evaporation
   d. continental deflection

   Answer: C Difficulty: 1 Section: 1 Objective: 4

9. As water gets denser, how does it move?
   a. expands toward warmer water
   b. sinks toward the ocean floor
   c. gets pushed toward the poles
   d. gets pulled up by evaporation

   Answer: B Difficulty: 1 Section: 1 Objective: 4

10. Which currents carry warm water away from the equator?
    a. deep currents
    b. evaporation
    c. surface currents
    d. freezing

    Answer: C Difficulty: 1 Section: 1 Objective: 1, 4

11. The two main parts of a wave are the
    a. swell and whitecap.
    b. wavelength and wave height.
    c. crest and trough.
    d. rise and dip.

    Answer: C Difficulty: 1 Section: 3 Objective: 1

12. As energy moves in waves through the water, the water moves
    a. in waves toward shore.
    b. in a small vertical circle.
    c. in the direction of the waves.
    d. against the current.

    Answer: A   Difficulty: 1   Section: 3   Objective: 3

13. When deep-water waves reach water shallower than one-half of their wavelength, they
    a. reverse their flow.
    b. enter the breaker zone.
    c. decrease in height.
    d. increase in height.

    Answer: D   Difficulty: 1   Section: 3   Objective: 2

14. What causes breakers to crash into the ocean floor?
    a. deep-water waves
    b. gravity
    c. short wavelengths
    d. shore currents

    Answer: B   Difficulty: 1   Section: 3   Objective: 3

15. Where does an undertow take sand and other particles from the shore?
    a. higher up on the shore
    b. as far as the first breaker
    c. out to sea
    d. farther on down the shore

    Answer: C   Difficulty: 1   Section: 3   Objective: 3

16. What transports most of the sediment in beach environments?
    a. undertows
    b. breakers
    c. longshore currents
    d. wind

    Answer: C   Difficulty: 1   Section: 3   Objective: 3

17. In the open ocean, whitecaps often form
    a. in places close to the shore.
    b. during storms.
    c. in warm-water currents.
    d. after swells go by.

    Answer: B   Difficulty: 1   Section: 3   Objective: 4

18. Which type of wave makes for the best sailing on the ocean?
    a. whitecaps
    b. tsunamis
    c. breakers
    d. swells

    Answer: D   Difficulty: 1   Section: 3   Objective: 4

19. A tsunami occurs when a large volume of water suddenly
    a. moves up and down.
    b. forms a giant wave.
    c. gets sucked below the surface.
    d. turns hotter or colder.

    Answer: B   Difficulty: 1   Section: 3   Objective: 4

20. What are the most destructive parts of hurricanes?
    a. tsunamis
    b. winds
    c. storm surges
    d. breakers

    Answer: C   Difficulty: 1   Section: 3   Objective: 4

21. In 1947 Thor Heyerdahl sailed a simple raft from Peru to Polynesia, following the ocean currents for more than 6,000 kilometers. Which statement accurately describes up what Heyerdahl proved by this voyage?
    a. Ancient Peru was settled by people from Polynesia.
    b. People from ancient Peru were the first settlers of Polynesia.
    c. It would have been possible for people from ancient Peru to reach Polynesia by following ocean currents.
    d. Polynesia was settled accidentally when rafts from Peru were carried out by ocean currents.

    Answer: C   Difficulty: 1   Section: 1   Objective: 1

22. Surface ocean currents such as Gulf Stream
    a. move warm water from higher latitudes to lower latitudes.
    b. transport many times more water than all the rivers in the world.
    c. are formed in parts of the ocean where water density is great.
    d. move in straight paths across the oceans.
    Answer: B   Difficulty: 1   Section: 1   Objective: 1

23. In which direction do global winds blow ocean currents near the equator?
    a. from east to west   c. counterclockwise
    b. from west to east   d. away from the poles
    Answer: A   Difficulty: 1   Section: 1   Objective: 2

24. Trying to roll a ball straight across a turning merry-go-round is a demonstration of what happens in the
    a. movement of global winds across the surface of the ocean.
    b. flow of currents and countercurrents at the equator.
    c. Coriolis effect.
    d. deflection of a current against a continent.
    Answer: C   Difficulty: 1   Section: 1   Objective: 2

25. Which surface current is deflected by the continent of South America?
    a. California Current   c. Brazil Current
    b. Labrador Current   d. North Equatorial Current
    Answer: C   Difficulty: 1   Section: 1   Objective: 2

26. Compared with surface currents, deep currents are
    a. colder and less dense.   c. warmer and denser.
    b. warmer and less dense.   d. colder and denser.
    Answer: D   Difficulty: 1   Section: 1   Objective: 3

27. When the air above water gets cold, what happens to water molecules?
    a. The water molecules evaporate, decreasing the water's density.
    b. The molecules slow down and move closer together, increasing the water's density.
    c. The water's volume increases as molecules move closer together.
    d. The denser water floats on top of the chilled water.
    Answer: B   Difficulty: 1   Section: 1   Objective: 4

28. Which of the following causes water from deep currents to rise to the surface to replace warm currents?
    a. the flow of warm currents from the equator toward the poles
    b. freezing of the surface of the water
    c. increased salinity due to evaporation
    d. squeezing solids out of the ice down into the water below
    Answer: C   Difficulty: 1   Section: 1   Objective: 4

29. How do warm-water currents affect the coastal areas along which they flow?
    a. They create greater rainfall along the coast.
    b. They create unusually cool climates for the latitude.
    c. They create unusually warm climates for the latitude.
    d. They make the coastal climate cooler than the inland climate.
    Answer: C   Difficulty: 1   Section: 2   Objective: 1

30. Which statement describes the negative effects of El Niño?
    a. El Nîño appears every 2 to 12 years.
    b. Rain, flash floods, and mudslides occur in places where there is usually little rain, while usually wet areas suffer from drought.
    c. Sometimes El Niño is followed by La Niña, during which ocean temperatures become cooler.
    d. Upwelling along the coast of South America occurs after an El Niño.
    Answer: B   Difficulty: 1   Section: 2   Objective: 2

31. It is important for scientists to learn as much as possible about El Niño because the weather pattern
    a. has so far been completely unpredictable.
    b. affects North America more than any other continent.
    c. has so many effects on organisms and land.
    d. can only be studied out in the open ocean.
    Answer: C   Difficulty: 1   Section: 2   Objective: 3

32. How do you calculate wave speed?
    a. Divide the wave period by the wavelength.
    b. Divide the wavelength by the wave period.
    c. Divide the wave height by the wave period.
    d. Multiply the wavelength by the wave height.
    Answer: B   Difficulty: 1   Section: 3   Objective: 2

33. Why do waves increase in height as they approach the shore?
    a. The waves are forced into narrow inlets of land.
    b. The water particles speed up as they approach land.
    c. The water's density decreases because it's warmer near the shore.
    d. The waves begin to interact with the ocean floor.
    Answer: D   Difficulty: 1   Section: 3   Objective: 3

34. In what direction does an undertow flow?
    a. in the same direction of the wave
    b. at right angles to the wave
    c. in the opposite direction as the wave
    d. parallel to the wave
    Answer: C   Difficulty: 1   Section: 3   Objective: 3

35. An earthquake causes a tsunami because force from the quake
    a. pushes a large body of water up from the ocean floor.
    b. pulls water down toward the source of the quake.
    c. blows surface water away from the shore.
    d. meets the force of currents flowing in a different direction.
    Answer: A   Difficulty: 1   Section: 3   Objective: 4

36. Which statement describes what is happening at high tide?
    a. The moon is revolving more quickly than the Earth is rotating.
    b. The moon's gravity is dragging water away from the equator.
    c. The moon's gravity is pulling ocean water into a bulge.
    d. The sun's gravity pulls with more force than the moon's gravity.
    Answer: C   Difficulty: 1   Section: 4   Objective: 4

37. Which statement explains why the moon's gravity is able to create high and low tides?
    a. The moon is revolving more quickly than the Earth is rotating.
    b. The moon is revolving more slowly than the Earth is rotating.
    c. Some parts of the Earth never face directly on the sun and moon.
    d. The moon is revolving at the same speed that the Earth is rotating.
    Answer: B   Difficulty: 1   Section: 4   Objective: 1

38. Spring tides and neap tides occur in patterns governed by
    a. changes in the force of the Earth's gravity.
    b. the type of ocean currents near where the tides occur.
    c. whether the gravity of the sun or moon exerts a stronger pull.
    d. the relative positions of the Earth, moon, and sun (the phases of the moon).
    Answer: D   Difficulty: 1   Section: 4   Objective: 2

39. From what is known about spring tides and neap tides, you can conclude that
    a. the sun's gravity exerts the most power when the moon is on the opposite side of the
       Earth from the sun.
    b. the height of high tides varies with the phases of the moon.
    c. spring tides and neap tides affect the phases of the moon.
    d. the moon revolves around the Earth every 14 days.
    Answer: B   Difficulty: 1   Section: 4   Objective: 2

40. A tidal bore is most likely to occur along a coast that has
    a. lower than usual tidal ranges.
    b. both warm- and cold-water currents offshore.
    c. narrow bays, inlets, and river channels.
    d. landforms that deflect the currents.
    Answer: C   Difficulty: 1   Section: 4   Objective: 3

41. How do changes in the circulation of ocean currents affect climate?
    a. by changing the atmosphere   c. by increasing salinity
    b. by moving water clockwise   d. by changing the tides
    Answer: A   Difficulty: 1   Section: 2   Objective: 1

42. Which event does NOT happen as the result of an upwelling?
    a. Cold-water currents replace warm-water currents.
    b. Surface currents flow away from the shore.
    c. The California Current moves water south from the North Pacific.
    d. Plants get the minerals they need for photosynthesis.
    Answer: C   Difficulty: 1   Section: 2   Objective: 1

43. If the wavelength of a wave stays the same, what happens when the wave period
    increases?
    a. increase in wave speed   c. decrease in wave speed
    b. increase in wave height   d. decrease in wave height
    Answer: C   Difficulty: 1   Section: 3   Objective: 2

44. Which of the following is most likely to spread pollution along the shore?
    a. upwelling 3   c. undertow
    b. breaker   d. longshore current
    Answer: D   Difficulty: 1   Section: 3   Objective: 3

45. When do the greatest tidal ranges occur?
    a. spring tides   c. high tides
    b. neap tides   d. low tides
    Answer: A   Difficulty: 1   Section: 4   Objective: 1

46. Which phrase describes a surface current?
    a. gets cool near the equator   c. stretches from north to south
    b. flows like a stream   d. creates global winds
    Answer: B   Difficulty: 1   Section: 1   Objective: 1

47. In what direction do global winds and currents flow near the equator?
    a. east to west   c. toward the land
    b. west to east   d. north to south
    Answer: A   Difficulty: 1   Section: 1   Objective: 1

48. How does the Coriolis effect make ocean currents appear to move?
    a. back and forth
    b. in a curved path
    c. clockwise
    d. against the Earth's rotation
    Answer: B   Difficulty: 1   Section: 1   Objective: 2

49. What happens to an ocean current when it hits a continent?
    a. It changes direction.
    b. It moves toward the poles.
    c. It moves toward the equator.
    d. It speeds up.
    Answer: A   Difficulty: 1   Section: 1   Objective: 2

50. How are deep currents different from surface currents?
    a. They are warmer and faster.
    b. They are caused by winds.
    c. They are denser and slower.
    d. Some are colder than others.
    Answer: C   Difficulty: 1   Section: 1   Objective: 3

51. What happens to water when the air above it gets cold?
    a. It evaporates.
    b. It slows down and cools.
    c. It moves faster to stay warm.
    d. Its salinity increases.
    Answer: B   Difficulty: 1   Section: 1   Objective: 4

52. What happens to the water that is left behind after evaporation?
    a. It gets hotter.
    b. It gets less dense.
    c. It moves faster to stay warm.
    d. Its salinity increases.
    Answer: D   Difficulty: 1   Section: 1   Objective: 4

53. What is the highest point of a wave?
    a. crest
    b. trough
    c. wave height
    d. wavelength
    Answer: A   Difficulty: 1   Section: 3   Objective: 1

54. What is the lowest point of a wave?
    a. crest
    b. trough
    c. wave height
    d. wavelength
    Answer: B   Difficulty: 1   Section: 3   Objective: 1

55. What is the distance between two crests or troughs?
    a. crest
    b. trought
    c. wave height
    d. wavelength
    Answer: D   Difficulty: 1   Section: 3   Objective: 1

56. What is the vertical distance between a crest and a trough?
    a. crest
    b. trought
    c. wave height
    d. wavelength
    Answer: C   Difficulty: 1   Section: 3   Objective: 1

57. The Gulf Stream Current moves warm water from
    a. Peru to Polynesia.
    b. higher to lower latitudes.
    c. lower to higher latitudes.
    d. east to west.
    Answer: C   Difficulty: 2   Section: 1   Objective: 2

58. Which continent deflects the Gulf Stream Current?
    a. North America
    b. South America
    c. Africa
    d. Asia
    Answer: A   Difficulty: 2   Section: 1   Objective: 2

59. What force makes cold water sink toward the ocean floor?
    a. global winds
    b. the sun
    c. gravity
    d. the Coriolis effect
    Answer: C   Difficulty: 3   Section: 1   Objective: 3

60. Which of these events happens first?
    a. The dense water sinks.
    b. The water travels as a deep current.
    c. The molecules move closer together.
    d. Cold air chills water molecules.
    Answer: D   Difficulty: 2   Section: 1   Objective: 4

61. What replaces a cold current that sinks to the ocean floor?
    a. a colder deep current   c. a colder surface current
    b. a warmer surface current   d. a slower surface current
    Answer: B   Difficulty: 2   Section: 1   Objective: 4

62. If ocean currents have changed their circulation patterns, you can conclude that
    a. patterns of wind circulation have also changed.
    b. the water is colder and denser than usual.
    c. the rate of evaporation has increased.
    d. the climate will be milder than usual.
    Answer: A   Difficulty: 2   Section: 2   Objective: 1

63. How would California be different if there were no California Current?
    a. Its climate would be cooler.
    b. There would be less wind and fog.
    c. Its climate would be drier.
    d. Its climate would be warmer.
    Answer: D   Difficulty: 2   Section: 2   Objective: 1

64. Which of these statements is NOT true about nutrients from the ocean floor?
    a. They include iron and nitrate.
    b. Tiny plants and animals depend on them.
    c. They are in the same food chains as fish.
    d. They get carried away from shore during an upwelling.
    Answer: D   Difficulty: 2   Section: 2   Objective: 1

65. What happens because El Niño damages a coral reef?
    a. The ocean water gets warmer.
    b. Fish that depend on the reef die.
    c. The ocean water gets cooler.
    d. The reef supports more diversity of life.
    Answer: B   Difficulty: 2   Section: 2   Objective: 2

66. Buoys that record El Niño can transmit data to satellites in space. What can you conclude from this fact?
    a. The buoy and its satellite are launched at the same time.
    b. The buoys are spread out along the equator.
    c. Scientists work and live on the buoys.
    d. The buoys are equipped with computers.
    Answer: D   Difficulty: 2   Section: 2   Objective: 3

67. How often do tides rise and fall?
    a. once a day   c. every 14 days
    b. twice a day   d. every 24 h, 50 m
    Answer: B   Difficulty: 3   Section: 4   Objective: 1

68. How often do neap tides occur?
    a. twice a month   c. with every full moon
    b. twice a day   d. twice every 28 days
    Answer: D   Difficulty: 2   Section: 4   Objective: 2

69. Which of these is the longest period of time?
    a. the time between high and low tides
    b. the time between two high tides
    c. the time between two spring tides
    d. the time between the highest and lowest tidal ranges
    Answer: C   Difficulty: 2   Section: 4   Objective: 3

70. Which of these takes exactly 24 h?
    a. one rotation of the Earth
    b. one revolution of the moon around the Earth
    c. one period between two high tides
    d. one period between two full moons
    Answer: A   Difficulty: 1   Section: 4   Objective: 1

71. The Bay of Fundy has the greatest tidal ranges on Earth. What can you infer about the Bay of Fundy?
    a. It faces the moon more often than other places on Earth.
    b. It has many rocky beaches.
    c. It is a long, narrow inlet.
    d. Its tides cannot be predicted accurately.
    Answer: C   Difficulty: 2   Section: 4   Objective: 3

COMPLETION

Use the terms from the following list to complete the sentences below.

Coriolis effect	deep currents
El Niño	surface currents
tides	tidal range
tsunami	upwelling
wavelength	

72. Although they flow near the top of the ocean, ___________________ can ocean reach depths of several hundred meters.
    Answer: surface currents
                       Difficulty: 1   Section: 1   Objective: 1

73. Although they flow near the bottom of the ocean, ___________________ sometimes flow on top of other currents.
    Answer: deep currents
                       Difficulty: 1   Section: 1   Objective: 1

74. The negative effects of ___________________ include flash floods, mudslides, and droughts.
    Answer: El Niño   Difficulty: 1   Section: 2   Objective: 2

75. The ___________________ is used to measure wave periods and therefore wave speed.
    Answer: wavelength   Difficulty 2   Section: 3   Objective: 2

76. The difference between levels of ocean water at high tide and low tide is called a(n) ___________________.
    Answer: tidal range   Difficulty: 1   Section: 4   Objective: 2

Use the terms from the following list to complete the sentences below.

breakers   tides
moon   tsunamis
tidal bore   wave period

77. A measurement of the time between two waves is called a ___________________.
    Answer: wave period
    Difficulty: 1   Section: 3   Objective: 2

78. Waves that build up and then crash into the ocean floor are known as

    ___________________.

    Answer: breakers   Difficulty: 1   Section: 3   Objective: 3

79. Huge waves called ___________________ are caused by underwater earthquakes,
    volcanic eruptions, and landslides.
    Answer: tsunamis   Difficulty: 1   Section: 3   Objective: 4

80. The most important force that creates tides is the gravity of the ___________________.
    Answer: moon   Difficulty: 1   Section: 4   Objective: 1

81. Neap, spring, high, and low are all types of ___________________.
    Answer: tides   Difficulty: 1   Section: 4   Objective: 2

82. A narrow inlet of land along a coast is where you might see a ___________________.
    This causes a very sudden rise in the tide.
    Answer: tidal bore   Difficulty: 1   Section: 4   Objective: 3

SHORT ANSWER

83. What three factors control surface currents?
    Answer: global winds, the Coriolis effect, continental deflections
    Difficulty: 1   Section: 4   Objective: 2

84. What are three factors that control deep currents?
    Answer: density, salinity, and temperature; accept also the Coriolis effect.
    Difficulty: 2   Section: 1   Objective: 4

85. What forms of technology are scientists using to study El Niño?
    Answer: buoys, satellites
    Difficulty: 1   Section: 2   Objective: 3

86. Explain why waves break as they reach the shore.
    Answer:
       As deep-water waves become shallow-water waves, the water particles slow down
       and build up. This change forces more water between wave crests, which increases
       wave height.
    Difficulty: 2   Section: 3   Objective: 3

87. Explain how the positions of the Earth, moon, and sun affect the tides.
    Answer:
    During spring tides, the gravity of the sun and pull on the Earth either from the same
       direction or from opposite directions, producing higher tidal ranges. During neap
       tides, the sun and moon are at right angles with respect to Earth. This lessens their pull
       on Earth, producing lower tidal ranges.
    Difficulty: 2   Section: 4   Objective: 1

88. Extra-large breakers are crashing into the surf. How will this effect the undertow? Make a prediction.
    Answer: The undertow will flow out to sea with more force than usual.
    Difficulty: 3   Section: 3   Objective: 3

89. Why do the majority of tsunamis occur in the Pacific Ocean?
    Answer: There are a lot of earthquakes in and around the Pacific Ocean.
    Difficulty: 2   Section: 3   Objective: 3

90. How do longshore currents shape the land?
    Answer:
       Longshore currents both tear down and build up the coastline by moving sand and sediments along the shore.
    Difficulty: 2   Section: 3   Objective: 4

91. Where and when do whitecaps form?
    Answer: Whitecaps form in the open ocean, usually during storms.
    Difficulty: 2   Section: 4   Objective: 4

92. Where is a storm surge located, in relation to the storm?
    Answer: A storm surge occurs under a storm.
    Difficulty: 2   Section: 3   Objective: 3

93. Compare rivers and surface currents.
    Answer:
       Both rivers and surface currents are long, moving bodies of water. However, rivers flow because of the pull of gravity, while surface currents are driven by the wind and by the rotation of the Earth.
    Difficulty: 2   Section: 1   Objective: 1, 2

94. Do global winds directly cause deep currents?
    Answer: no
    Difficulty: 1   Section: 1   Objective: 3

95. Can ocean currents be caused by differences in water temperature?
    Answer: yes
    Difficulty: 2   Section: 1   Objective: 3

96. Can ocean currents be caused by differences in salinity?
    Answer: yes
    Difficulty: 1   Section: 1   Objective: 4

97. Give two characteristics and one example of each type of current.
    Answer:
       Sample answer: Surface currents occur at the surface of the ocean are caused by global winds; the Gulf Stream is an example. Deep currents occur deep in the ocean and are influenced by water density, salinity, and temperature. The Antarctic Bottom Water is an example.
    Difficulty: 2   Section: 1   Objective: 4

98. Explain how ocean temperatures affect the climate of coastal cities.
    Answer:
       The ocean's ability to retain warmth keeps the temperatures of coastal areas generally milder than temperatures of inland areas nearby.
    Difficulty: 2   Section: 2   Objective: 1

99. You are floating on the ocean 1 km from shore, which is north of you. A surface current is flowing east. Are you more likely to travel north with the waves toward the shore or east with the surface current?

Answer:

   East, because wave energy travels through the water, but the water doesn't travel with the waves.

   Difficulty: 2   Section: 3   Objective: 3

100. Why might sighting a line of offshore breakers cause sailors to turn their boats around?

Answer:

   As water becomes shallower, the wave height increases and the waves may break. Breaking waves could signal a submerged sandbar or reef and a ship could run aground.

   Difficulty: 2   Section: 3   Objective: 4

MATCHING

a. California Current	f. La Niña
b. cold-water	g. buoys
c. drought	h. Tropics
d. El Niño	i. upwelling
e. Gulf Stream	j. warm-water

101. ____ type of current that creates warmer climates in coastal areas

   Answer: B   Difficulty: 1   Section: 2   Objective: 1

102. ____ type of current that creates cooler climates in coastal areas

   Answer: J   Difficulty: 1   Section: 2   Objective: 1

103. ____ where the Gulf Stream and other warm currents originate

   Answer: H   Difficulty: 1   Section: 2   Objective: 1

104. ____ ocean current that warms the British Isles

   Answer: E   Difficulty: 1   Section: 2   Objective: 1

105. ____ ocean current that cools the West Coast of the United States

   Answer: A   Difficulty: 1   Section: 2   Objective: 1

106. ____ the movement of cold, nutrient-rich water to the surface of the ocean

   Answer: I   Difficulty: 1   Section: 2   Objective: 1

107. ____ a change in the water temperature of the Pacific Ocean that produces a warm current

   Answer: D   Difficulty: 1   Section: 2   Objective: 2

108. ____ a change in the water temperature of the eastern Pacific Ocean that produces cooler than usual surface water temperatures

   Answer: F   Difficulty: 1   Section: 2   Objective: 2

109. ____ an unusually long period during which rainfall is below average

   Answer: C   Difficulty: 1   Section: 2   Objective: 2

110. ____ used to collect data to predict an El Niño

   Answer: G   Difficulty: 1   Section: 2   Objective: 3

a. gravity	f. spring tide
b. high tide	g. sun
c. low tide	h. tidal bore
d. moon	i. tidal range
e. neap tide	j. tides

111. ____ the periodic daily rise and fall of ocean water

   Answer: J   Difficulty: 1   Section: 4   Objective: 1

112. ____ the force that pulls the tides

    Answer: A   Difficulty: 1   Section: 4   Objective: 1

113. ____ main source of gravity for tides

    Answer: D   Difficulty: 1   Section: 4   Objective: 1

114. ____ bulge that takes place on parts of Earth facing or opposite the moon

    Answer: B   Difficulty: 1   Section: 4   Objective: 2

115. ____ forms when water is drawn away from the area between high tides

    Answer: C   Difficulty: 1   Section: 4   Objective: 2

116. ____ celestial body around which Earth rotates

    Answer: G   Difficulty: 1   Section: 4   Objective: 1

117. ____ the difference between water levels at low and high tide

    Answer: I   Difficulty: 1   Section: 4   Objective: 2

118. ____ tides that occur during the new and full moons

    Answer: F   Difficulty: 1   Section: 4   Objective: 2

119. ____ tides that occur during the first and third quarters of the moon

    Answer: E   Difficulty: 1   Section: 4   Objective: 2

120. ____ a body of water that rushes into a narrow bay and causes a very sudden tidal rise

    Answer: H   Difficulty: 1   Section: 4   Objective: 3

a. crest
b. current
c. swell
d. trough
e. wavelength
f. wave height

121. ____ the lowest part of a wave

    Answer: D   Difficulty: 1   Section: 3   Objective: 1

122. ____ the highest part of a wave

    Answer: A   Difficulty: 1   Section: 3   Objective: 1

123. ____ the vertical distance between the highest and lowest points of a wave

    Answer: F   Difficulty: 1   Section: 3   Objective: 1

124. ____ the vertical difference between two adjacent high points or two adjacent low points
     of a wave

    Answer: E   Difficulty: 1   Section: 3   Objective: 1

a. California Current
b. climate
c. Gulf Stream
d. upwelling

125. ____ current that flows south to cool the West Coast of the United States

    Answer: A   Difficulty: 1   Section: 2   Objective: 1

126. ____ a long-term weather pattern that can be changed by an ocean current

    Answer: B   Difficulty: 1   Section: 2   Objective: 1

127. ____ current that carries water from the Tropics to the British Isles

    Answer: C   Difficulty: 1   Section: 2   Objective: 1

128. ____ a rise of cold water from deep in the ocean to the warmer surface

    Answer: D   Difficulty: 1   Section: 2   Objective: 1

a. drought
b. El Niño
c. La Niña
d. buoys

129. ____ weather pattern that makes the ocean surface cooler

    Answer: C   Difficulty: 1   Section: 2   Objective: 2

130. ____ weather pattern that makes the ocean surface warmer

    Answer: B   Difficulty: 1   Section: 2   Objective: 2

131. ____ devices used to collect data to predict an El Niño

    Answer: D   Difficulty: 1   Section: 2   Objective: 3

132. ____ a long period of time with no rain

    Answer: A   Difficulty: 1   Section: 2   Objective: 2

a. depth	d. speed
b. distance	e. time
c. energy	f. volume

133. _____ what you would have to know to classify a wave as either a deep- or shallow-water wave

Answer: A   Difficulty: 2   Section: 3   Objective: 4

134. _____ what is measured by a wave period

Answer: E   Difficulty: 2   Section: 3   Objective: 2

135. _____ what moves through water and forms a wave

Answer: C   Difficulty: 2   Section: 3   Objective: 3

136. _____ what increases when a wave period decreases

Answer: D   Difficulty: 2   Section: 3   Objective: 3

137. _____ what wave height and wavelength measure

Answer: B   Difficulty: 2   Section: 3   Objective: 1

ESSAY

138. Do winds and currents flow faster at the equator than at the poles, or more slowly? Think about what you know regarding the shape and rotation of the Earth, the directions of currents, and convection. Make inferences from what you know. Then give reasons to support your answer.

Answer:

Winds and currents flow faster at the equator than at the poles. One reason equatorial currents are faster is that they are warmer. Another reason is that the speed of the Earth's rotation is much faster at the equator. (A point near the poles and a point at the equator both rotate in 24 hours, but the point at the equator has traveled a much greater distance in that time.)

Difficulty: 3   Section: 1   Objective: 2

139. El Niño can prevent upwelling along the Pacific Coast. What might happen if normal upwelling does not take place? Make predictions and support them with facts from the chapter.

Answer:

If El Niño prevents an upwelling, nutrients from the ocean floor are not brought up to the surface. This deprives tiny shore plants and animals of nutrients and harms the shoreline ecosystem.

Difficulty: 2   Section: 2   Objective: 2

140. How might a heavy undertow affect the formation of breakers above it? Use your answer to question 14 to form a hypothesis.

Answer:

Breakers form as waves interact with the ocean floor. Undertows are moving out to sea along the ocean floor. Therefore undertows must contribute to the slowing down of incoming waves and the buildup of water molecules that cause the waves to increase in height.

Difficulty: 2   Section: 3   Objective: 3

141. Why should people who live in coastal areas learn about currents, waves, and tides? Give examples of how waves and tides could affect everyday lives.

Answer:

People in coastal areas should learn about tides and waves in order to predict the best times for using the beach, to prevent accidents, and to stay alert for dangers, such as storm surges.

Difficulty: 2   Section: 3   Objective: 4

CONCEPT MAPPING

142. Use the following terms to complete the concept map below:

> breakers
> surf
> undertow
>
> deep-water waves
> swells

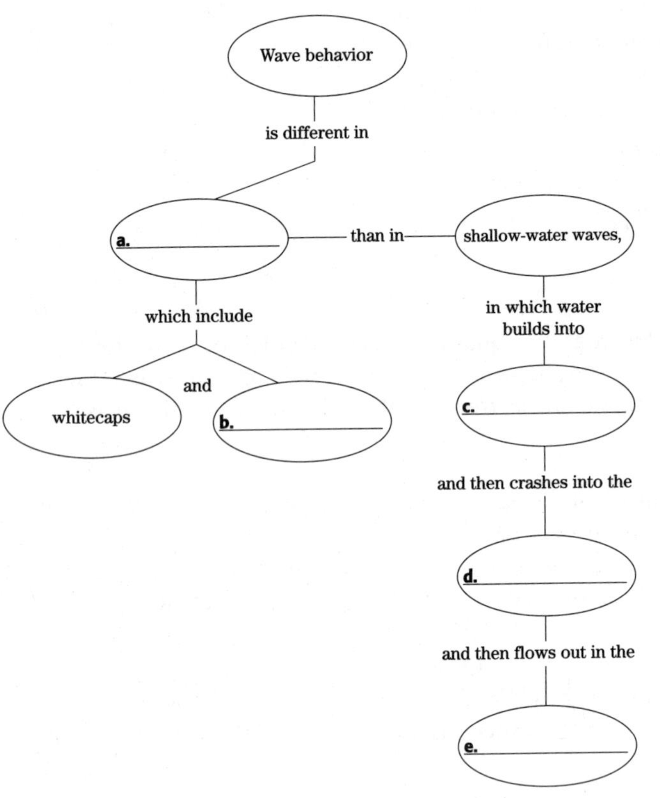

Answer:
a. deep-water waves; b. swells; c. breakers; d. surf; e. undertow

Difficulty: 3   Section: 3   Objective: 4

TRUE/FALSE

Tell whether each of these statements is true or false.

143. _____ Upwelling is a process in which warm, nutrient-rich water from the deep ocean rises to the surface.
Answer: False Difficulty: 1 Section: 2 Objective: 1

144. _____ El Niño occurs every 2 to 12 years.
Answer: True Difficulty: 1 Section: 2 Objective: 2`

145. _____ During an El Niño, California usually experiences a drought.
Answer: False Difficulty: 2 Section: 2 Objective: 2

146. _____ Surface currents greatly affect the climate in many parts of the world.
Answer: True Difficulty: 1 Section: 2 Objective: 1

9997282094   2 3 4 5 6